Build Your Own Furniture

20 DESIGNS

Build Your Own Furniture:

20 Designs

Peter Stamberg

Photographs by Paul Warchol and William P. Steele

BALLANTINE BOOKS • NEW YORK

Designs 1, 8, 10, and 11 originally appeared in *House & Garden*.

Cover photographs:
Front cover: Karen Radkai (top center); Paul Warchol/ESTO. Copyright © 1980 by Paul Warchol (top left and right, bottom lower left, lower right, and center); William P. Steele (bottom upper left and upper right). *Back cover:* William P. Steele (top left and right); Paul Warchol/ESTO. Copyright © 1980 by Paul Warchol (bottom left and right).

Color insert photographs:
Design 1; Design 11: Peter Stamberg.
Design 8 (3 photos); Design 10 (3 photos): Photographer William P. Steele. Courtesy *House & Garden.* Copyright © 1979 by The Condé Nast Publications Inc.
All other photographs: Copyright © 1980 by Paul Warchol

Library of Congress Catalog Card Number: 81-66174

ISBN 0-345-29553-6

Manufactured in the United States of America

Typographic design by Julie M. Barnes

First Edition: September 1981

10 9 8 7 6 5 4 3 2 1

Acknowledgments

The governing principle behind the simple construction technique employed in the assembly of all the designs contained in this book grew out of discussions between Dino Gavina and myself in June 1974. This first encounter with Gavina totally changed my approach to design. Gavina spoke of a need to build on the foundations laid by Marcel Breuer in his landmark designs of the 1920s. From these rather serious discussions came the simple, perhaps humble, yet in some ways sophisticated designs in this book. My greatest hope is that my work truly reflects the traditions and excellence that underlie all the projects initiated by Dino Gavina. With respect and admiration, my thanks go to Dino Gavina.

In addition, I would like to thank members of the group that surrounds Gavina for their inspiration: the clear-minded Kazuhide Takahama; Maria Simoncini; Enzo Mari, to whose example I owe a great debt; and the late architect Carlo Scarpa, whose work will inspire many in generations to come.

I would also like to express my gratitude to a number of people who have helped bring the seed of this book to flower: my parents, Lois and Mel Stamberg, for their support; my sister and brother, Jill and Al Jarnow, for their inspiration and technical help; Jean Koefoed, for his unhesitating support and practical, inspired guidance; Beverly Russell, for her faith in my ability to get things done well and promptly; Claire Whitcomb, for her invaluable help in preparing the instructions and stories for the features in *House and Garden;* Ivory Tower and Michael Wager, my clients, patrons, and friends, for the use of their homes as photography locations; Paul Warshol, for his wonderful photographs and generosity with his time; Karen Radkai and Bill Steele, for the marvelous photographs that they took of my work for *House and Garden;* Rick, Dorothy, and Stephen Globus, for their encouragement over the years; Amy Berkhower, Dan Weiss, and Jeffrey Weiss, for their selfless advice; Jim Wegeler, for his handling of things which I could never; Joelle Delbourgo, of Ballantine Books, for her encouragement, patience, and enthusiasm; and Susan Long, for help with the drawings. Finally, and most importantly, my unending gratitude goes to Paul Aferiat, whose own high standards and impeccable judgment helped me to maintain the integrity which you will, I hope, find in the following designs.

Contents

Accessories

Glossary

Preface

If you've shopped for furniture lately, you probably were astonished at the high price tags most pieces carry. As furniture prices continue to soar, you may envision yourself living in barren surroundings—with nothing between the ceiling and floor.

Now there's an alternative to getting by without the furnishings you need or to straining your budget to buy the furniture of your dreams. Whatever your needs and style, *Build Your Own Furniture* will help you get the look you want in your home and office—at a price that you can afford.

This step-by-step guide to building flexible, contemporary designs will take you from the basics, like tables and chairs, to accessories, such as a wine rack or flower box. All of the designs are relatively easy to build, attractive, and durable. And most of them can be built for under $50, many for less than $5, using the best materials available.

Best of all, you don't have to be a master carpenter to use this book. If you've never driven a nail into a piece of wood, you can follow "The Carpentry Guide" (page 1), for tips on buying materials, building techniques, and finishing touches. "Twenty Designs" follow, with easy instructions illustrated every step of the way. The "Glossary" on page 113 will help you to master carpentry terms. And you can turn to the color section to see what the finished designs look like in a variety of different settings.

Whether you want to furnish your home from A to Z, to replace hand-me-down furnishings with pieces you really like, or to brighten up your quarters with exciting accessories, *Build Your Own Furniture* will meet your need and budget—in just hours!

—Peter Stamberg

Design #	Description	Approximate Assembly Time	Cost of Materials	Complexity
1	Folding Chair	2 hrs.	$ 10.00	3
2	C.C. Modular	3 hrs.	*$ 13.00	4
3	34-Inch-Square Table	4 hrs.	$ 25.00	3
4	Dining Table	3 hrs.	$ 35.00	3
5	Occasional Table	2 hrs.	$ 8.00	2
6	Snack Table	2 hrs.	$ 8.00	3
7	Four-Poster Bed	3 days	*$200.00	4
8	Free-Standing Shelves	5 hrs.	$ 45.00	4
9	Small Wall Unit	2 hrs.	$ 8.00	2
10	Small Storage Column	1½ hrs.	$ 15.00	2
11	Tall Storage Column	2 hrs.	$ 40.00	2
12	18-Inch Towel Bar	1 hr.	$ 2.50	1
13	24-Inch Towel Bar	1 hr.	$ 2.80	1
14	36-Inch Towel Bar	1 hr.	$ 2.95	1
15	Wall Hooks	½ hr.	$ 2.00	1
16	Letter Holder	½ hr.	$ 1.20	1
17	Wine Rack	2 hrs.	$ 20.00	2
18	Coat Stand	4 hrs.	$ 20.00	3
19	Dressing Screen	4 hrs.	$ 35.00	2
20	Plant Box	2 hrs.	$ 5.00	2

*Plus upholstery

The chart above illustrates the approximate cost, assembly time, and level of complexity of the designs in *Build Your Own Furniture*. Costs and assembly time will vary, of course, with local prices and the pace at which you prefer to work. Although the designs require no more than the most basic carpentry skills, they do vary somewhat in level of complexity. The designs are rated 1 (least complex) through 4 (most complex). A beginning carpenter might be wise to hammer and saw briefly among the 1's and 2's, developing his or her skills and confidence, before attempting the 3's and 4's.

Carpentry Guide

The Right Tools for the Job

The following is a guide to basic tools you'll need to construct the projects in *Build Your Own Furniture*. When buying tools you should shop for quality, not bargains. Good tools can last a lifetime and provide markedly better results, while cheap tools will break, chip, dull, and generally give you more trouble than the savings were worth. Bad tools also can be dangerous.

1. Hammer. The most basic tool for building is a curved-claw hammer. A good drop-forged hammer will be a worthwhile investment for a lifetime. Avoid the less expensive cast-iron hammers, which break easily and can chip, sending fragments into the eye. Hammers with steel or fiberglass handles are generally better than wood-handled hammers because wood handles can shrink if stored in a place that is too dry, causing the head to come off the handle.

2. Handsaws. Again, it pays to invest in a good saw. Cheap saws dull quickly and are difficult to resharpen. A dull saw is dangerous and can ruin wood by splintering it. A crosscut handsaw is the most basic type of general-purpose saw. A backsaw is somewhat smaller than a crosscut handsaw and may be better for the projects in this book. Because of its rigid back, it has less flexibility than the crosscut saw; many beginning carpenters find it easier to work with. The backsaw works well when used in conjunction with a miter box, which also ensures perfectly straight cuts. The fine teeth of the backsaw make very smooth cuts.

3. Power Saws. Probably the best type of power saw for projects in this book in terms of speed, accuracy, and ease of use is a small table saw. In my own shop I use a "Rockwell 9" Homecraft Saw." Craftsman, Sears' brand name for its own tools, also makes an excellent small table saw. Table saws generally come with an angle-adjustable guide that makes the cutting of angles other than 90 degrees very easy.

The most basic power saw, a portable circular saw, is a useful tool not only for the projects in this book but for many types of building projects. When buying a circular saw, make sure that it has both depth and angle adjustments that are easy to use. It should also have a spring-loaded blade guard that retracts by itself as the saw blade enters the wood and then springs back to cover the blade as soon as the cutting is complete. Because none of the projects in this book require you to cut anything thicker than ¾ inch, a 4½-inch trim saw will do a more than adequate job. Because of the trim saw's light weight and small size, it is quite easy to handle.

4. Power Drills. Aside from a hammer, a power drill is probably the most useful tool to own. In addition to drilling holes, with the right attachments you can use it to tighten screws, sand wood, stir paint, cut circles, cut metal, and even dig holes in the garden for planting bulbs. The largest size shank that a drill will accommodate determines its size. I use a ⅜-inch Rockwell drill. For larger holes, one can use an oversized drill bit with a cut-down shank.

In addition to Rockwell, both Sears' Craftsman and Black & Decker make very good drills. Whatever drill you buy should have a means of locking in the **on** position as well as a variable speed switch so that you can select the best speed for any purpose. Many drills are also reversible for ease in backing out of deep holes and for removing screws.

5. Combination Square. A combination square is useful for marking right angles and checking assemblies for squareness. As many combination squares also contain spirit levels, they can also ensure that horizontal surfaces are perfectly level and vertical surfaces are perfectly upright.

6. Carpenter's Square. Generally larger than either combination squares or try squares, carpenter's squares are used mainly to check for squareness in adjoining members and for marking measurements.

7. Steel Tape Ruler. A steel tape ruler is probably the best tool for measuring length, nail positioning, and spacing.

8. Screwdriver. Be sure to use the proper screwdriver for the screws at hand. If the screwdriver is too big, it obviously won't fit

into the slot on the head; if it is too small, it may strip the slot, making your job very difficult and messy.

9. Miter Box and Backsaw. If you use a handsaw rather than a power saw, a miter box and backsaw will give the best results for accuracy and smoothness.

10. Nail Set. Use a nail set to countersink finishing-nail heads below the wood surface.

11. Putty Knife. Use a putty knife to apply Plastic Wood for filling holes where nails have been countersunk.

12. Safety Equipment. Whenever sanding, whether with a power sander or by hand, you should always wear a mask to keep sawdust from getting in your mouth and nose. Goggles should be worn when working with power tools: sawdust, splinters, nail chips, and finishing materials are very dangerous to the eyes. Also, it's a good idea to wear gloves for protection whether you are hammering, sawing, sanding, gluing, or finishing wood. Disposable rubber gloves, useful for finishing wood, are inexpensive.

Materials

1. Wood. When buying wood, shop around: lumber prices vary from lumberyard to lumberyard, from week to week. One week a certain yard may have the best price, the next week another. Before you walk into a lumberyard, call a few, tell them what you need, and ask about prices. Also check the price for precutting if you plan to have the yard cut the wood to length for you.

Pine is the best type of wood for the projects in this book; it is also the most commonly available. Pine comes in many grades. Grading standards vary from area to area. Depending on your budget and the look you want, you should purchase either "No. 2 Pine" or "Clear Pine." However, whatever you buy should be "dressed four sides." Number 2 pine is considerably less

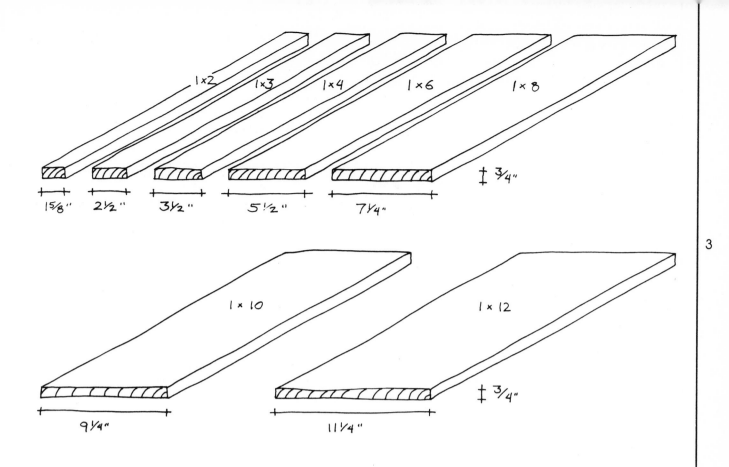

expensive than clear pine, but what some yards consider No. 2 is just about good enough for firewood. Real No. 2 will have occasional small, tight knots. These knots should never be more than one quarter to one third the width of the board and should be firmly in place. Larger knots will cause problems for two reasons: first, they are weak spots in the wood; and, second, nails should not be driven in or near them. With clear pine, there should be no knots, and the wood should be perfectly straight and smooth.

Inspect each piece of wood in the lumberyard. If you are not happy with it there, you will be less happy with it at home. The best quality gauge is your own eye. Wood that is black may be rotted. Wood that is green can have shrinkage and expansion problems later. Look down the edge of each board to make sure that you have a straight piece.

There is a significant difference between nominal wood sizes (what you will ask for) and actual wood sizes (what you will get). All the projects in this series are built with what are nominally called "one by's"—that is, 1 inch by 2 inches, 1 inch by 3 inches, 1 inch by 4 inches, etc. A piece that you will order as a 1 by 2 will actually be ¾ inch thick. Widths are a bit more tricky. A 1 x 2 should be 1⅝ inches wide but is sometimes as narrow as 1½ inches or as wide as 1¾ inches; 1 x 3 through 1 x 6 should be ½ inch less than nominal size; 1 x 8 through 1 x 12 are subject to great variation. The illustration above shows nominal versus actual dimensions.

2. Glue. I use Elmer's Professional Carpenter's wood glue. Made by Borden's, it is available in most lumberyards and hardware stores. If you cannot find it, any white glue, such as Elmer's Glue-All or Sobo will do just fine.

3. Nails. For the projects in this book, all you will need are 3-penny (abbreviated 3d) finishing nails (1¼ inches long) or 4-penny (4d) finishing nails (1½ inches long). Three-penny finishing nails are most commonly sold in hardware stores, where they may be called "1¼-inch wire brads." Wire brads come in several thicknesses or gauges; 15- or 16-gauge is recommended. Four-penny finishing nails are almost always available in both hardware stores and lumberyards.

One generally buys nails by the pound. One pound of 3-penny nails contains approximately 850 nails. One pound of 4-penny nails contains approximately 625 nails.

4. Nuts, Bolts, Washers. All projects in this series with moving parts require nuts, bolts, and washers (those little metal rings that fit between the nut and the bolt). All can be found in a hardware store and come with black or galvanized (silver-colored) finishes. Black hardware has a great look when contrasted against natural pine.

5. Sandpaper. Hardware stores and lumberyards sell sandpaper in small sheets. You will generally need medium grade for initial sanding and fine grade after that. Use finishing paper before applying the first coat of finish and between coats of clear finish. Make sure to remove dust before applying each coat of finish.

Finishing Materials

Finishing your furniture, whether you use paint or a clear finish, is a very simple job. However, you should take the time (and it can be time consuming) to do it properly. First, a high-quality brush is a good investment. No matter how good the brush is, be sure to remove loose bristles before use. I have also found the new sponge brushes for paint effective as well as economical.

Never finish pieces before they are glued together. Prefinishing may seem like a good way to save time and to finish those hard-to-get-at areas, but glue joints will not hold on paint or clear finish.

You can hide nail heads by countersinking nails; that is, driving the heads below the wood surface with a nail set. After countersinking, fill the small holes above the nail heads with Plastic Wood. Plastic Wood, available in most lumberyards and hardware stores, comes in several wood tones so that you can match it to your wood, should you use a clear finish. If you plan to apply a translucent stain to your furniture, the stain should be premixed with Plastic Wood for best results. With any finishing material (stain, dye, clear finish, or paint), always read the manufacturer's directions on the can.

Always use high-gloss paint for furniture. It prevents hand oils from seeping into wood and is also the only paint that will stand up to a thorough cleaning. Apply a primer coat before the color you have selected. The primer will save you money as well as give you a better end result. Primer costs less than pigmented paint. It will soak in and fill the wood so that your pigment will not be wasted as a filler. Also, paint applies more evenly over primer than over raw wood.

Hint: Since yellow has even less opacity than white, it is the most difficult pigment with which to get an even color. If you do wish to use yellow paint, make sure the wood is well primed. A second coat of primer or even a coat of white paint underneath the yellow will improve the finish. Though to a lesser extent, the same holds true for all pastel colors.

All primers have different drying times, so follow the directions on the can and be patient. If possible, avoid painting on rainy or extremely humid days. If, however, you have a piece of unfinished furniture staring at you on a rainy day and the urge to finish it is uncontrollable, allow even more drying time between coats than the manufacturer recommends.

Once the primer has dried thoroughly, apply your high-gloss enamel paint. Use enough paint for total coverage but not so much that the paint will drip or run. Two thin coats of paint are more desirable than one thick coat.

Wood can be lightened, darkened, or even colored by using stains and dyes, which you can find in paint stores. Directions for using these products vary greatly, so follow the manufacturer's directions.

The number of clear finishes on the market seems endless. Shellac, oil, varnish, and polyurethane varnish are the most common. Polyurethane is the most expensive but also the most durable. It is available in matte, semigloss, and high-gloss finishes. McCloskey's Kwik Sand and Heirloom finishes give fine results. The wood gains an excellent tone, which looks fresh, yet it is hard to tell whether the wood is new or aged. Benjamin Moore's interior satin, neutral blender, and hi-luster clear have a range of tones and colors large enough to satisfy many tastes. The finish you use, however, should be a "non-yellowing" product, which many are not.

Finally, every clear finish will darken wood and impart a slight yellowish cast when first applied. Test the finish you are about to use on an extra piece of wood or on a small hidden area. If you want light wood to stay light, you can use wood lightener or a bit of white stain. A properly selected wood lightener can lighten the wood with the first coat so that subsequent clear finishes will return it close to its natural color.

The Carpenter's Secrets: Six Hints

1. Blunting Nails. Before starting nails in finished carpentry, such as furniture assembly, you should blunt the point of the nails. Blunting the point reduces the chance of the wood splitting. You can blunt a nail point by placing the head of the nail on a hard surface (a piece of metal) and gently tapping the nail point with a hammer.

2. Holding the Hammer. Hold the hammer as close to the base as possible. Holding the hammer too close to the hammer head reduces the force of the hammer blow and angles the face of the hammer incorrectly, causing nails to go askew or bend. If the nail begins to bend or if the wood begins to split, stop nailing and start a new nail. If the wood is split, start the nail nearby but not in the line of the split, or else the wood will only split more.

3. Starting and Driving Nails. You should always start nails before applying glue. If you drive the nail into the first piece of wood far enough so that the point protrudes slightly through the other side, the pieces won't slide apart when you apply glue and hammer.

4. Where to Work. Always work on a hard surface. A soft surface, such as carpet, will absorb the force of the hammer and can also cause the wood to split. If you do not have a work table, here are two suggestions: work on a floor protected by a drop cloth, or work on a sheet of ¾-inch plywood on top of a solid table or sawhorses.

5. The Perfect Glue Joint. Among carpenters there is actually something known as the perfect glue joint; this is a connection in which the glue joint is stronger than the wood. To achieve a perfect glue joint, spread glue over the wood surface, entirely filling the area being joined, just inside the positioning marks. The pressure of the hammer will make the glue spread and seep out of all the edges. Wipe away excess glue immediately with a damp cloth or a damp paper towel, since many clear finishes will turn white and stains may discolor when applied over glue residue. Once the glue has dried completely, should you try to pull the glued joint apart, ideally the wood itself will break rather than the glue.

6. Outdoor Use. If you want to use your furniture outdoors, you should screw it together rather than using nails and glue. There are no glues for home use that are completely water resistant.

SEATING

Design 1:
The Folding Chair

Materials

Wood	• Eight 6-foot lengths of 1 x 13-inch pine
Hardware	• Eighty 4-penny finishing nails
	• Four ¼-inch wing nuts
	• Four ¼-by-2-inch carriage bolts
	• Eight ¼-inch washers
Glue	• Approximately one and one-half ounces of wood glue
Sandpaper	• One sheet of medium-grain sandpaper
	• One sheet of fine-grain sandpaper

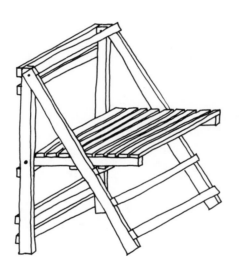

Step 1: Cut the wood to size.

☐ From one 6-foot length cut two pieces, each 35½ inches long.

☐ From each of two 6-foot lengths cut three pieces, one 30 inches and two 20 inches.

☐ From one 6-foot length cut two pieces, each 20½ inches.

☐ From each of two 6-foot lengths cut four pieces, two 18⁵⁄₁₆ inches and two 16¹¹⁄₁₆ inches.

☐ From one 6-foot length cut four pieces, one 18⁵⁄₁₆ inches and three 16¹¹⁄₁₆ inches.

☐ From one 6-foot length cut four pieces, each 16¹¹⁄₁₆ inches.

Step 2: Sand the wood.

Step 3: Assemble the diagonal unit.

☐ Place the two 35½-inch-long pieces together on the work surface, resting on their ¾-inch edges, and mark seven lines across each as shown.

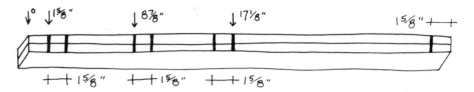

☐ Start four nails into each of the four 20-inch-long pieces, two nails at each end. The nails are each ½ inch in from the end and ⅜ inch in from the side edge.

☐ Place the two 35½-inch-long pieces parallel to one another on the work surface, resting on their ¾-inch edge, so that the distance from the outer edge of one to the outer edge of the other is 20 inches.

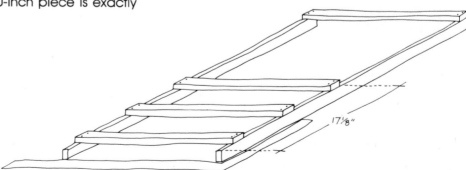

☐ One by one glue and nail the 20-inch-long pieces to the 35½-inch-long pieces. Position the 20-inch-long pieces according to the pencil marks. Make sure that the distance from the bottom end of the 35½-inch-long piece to the top edge of the third 20-inch piece is exactly 17⅛ inches.

Step 4: Assemble the vertical unit.

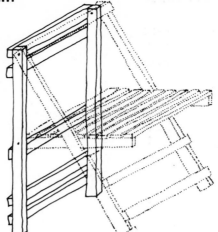

☐ Place the two 30-inch-long pieces together on the work surface, resting on their ¾-inch edges, and mark nine lines across each, as shown.

2¼" 1⅝" 3" 1⅝" 3" 1⅝"   1⅝" 3" 1⅝"

☐ Start four nails into each of the five 18⁵⁄₁₆-inch-long pieces, two at each end. The nails are each ½ inch in from the end and ⅜ inch from the side edge as before.

☐ Place the two 30-inch-long pieces parallel to one another on the work surface so that the distance from the outer edge of one to the outer edge of the other is 18⁵⁄₁₆ inches.

18⁵⁄₁₆"

☐ One by one, using the pencil lines as guides, glue and nail the five 18⁵⁄₁₆-inch-long pieces to the 30-inch-long pieces.

18⁵⁄₁₆"

Step 5: Assemble the seat unit.

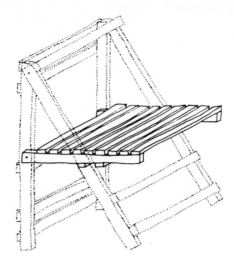

☐ Place the two 20½-inch-long pieces together on the work surface, resting on their ¾-inch edges, and mark seventeen lines across each. The first line is 1⅝ inches from either end. The second line is ⅜ inch from the first. The third line is 1⅝ inches from the second. The fourth is ⅜ inches from the third. Continue this sequence until you have marked 17 lines.

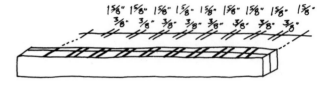

☐ Start four nails into each of the eleven 16¹¹⁄₁₆-inch-long pieces, positioned as in Step 3 and Step 4.

☐ Place the two 20½-inch-long pieces on the work surface, parallel to one another and resting on ¾-inch edges, so that the distance from the outer edge of one to the outer edge of the other is 16¹¹⁄₁₆ inches.

☐ One by one, glue and nail nine of the 16¹¹⁄₁₆-inch-long pieces to the 20½-inch-long pieces, using the pencil lines as placement guides.

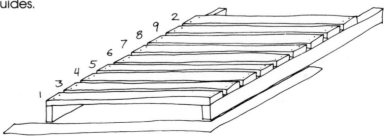

☐ Turn the seat unit over and mark four lines across each of the two 20½-inch-long pieces, as shown.

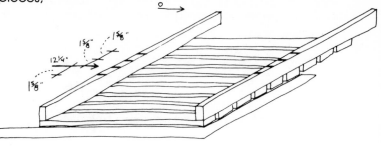

☐ Glue and nail the two remaining 16¹¹⁄₁₆-inch-long pieces to the 20½-inch-long pieces in the positions indicated by the pencil marks.

Step 6: Drill assembly holes.

☐ Mark four drilling points on the 30-inch-high vertical unit, two points on each 30-inch-long piece. One point on each side is ⅝ inch down from the top and the other is 16⅞ inches up from the bottom. The top holes are ⅝ inch from the front side, and the bottom holes are ½ inch from the front side.

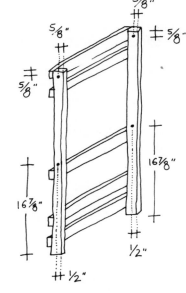

☐ Mark two drilling points on the 35½-inch-high diagonal unit, one on each 35½-inch-long piece. Both holes are ⅝ inch down from the top and ½ inch in from the edge as shown.

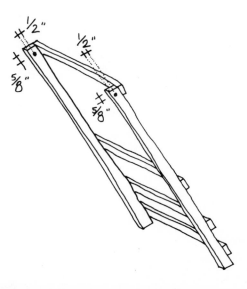

☐ Mark two drilling points on the seat unit, one on each 20½-inch-long piece. The holes are both ⅝ inch in from the end and ¹³⁄₁₆ inch up from the bottom, as shown.

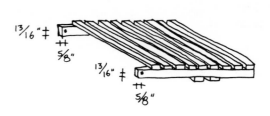

☐ Drill the eight holes as marked. Each hole is ¼ inch in diameter.

Step 7: Apply desired finishing material.

☐ Wait until the glue has dried thoroughly before applying finishing material. Wait until finishing material has dried before beginning final assembly.

Step 8: Complete final assembly.

☐ Attach the diagonal unit to the vertical unit using two carriage bolts, four washers, and two wing nuts. First insert one carriage bolt into each of the two holes in the top of the diagonal unit so that the carriage bolt protrudes about ⅛ inch through the far side of the hole. Hang one washer on protruding end of each carriage bolt. Position the vertical unit between the bolts and push the bolts through the holes in the top of the vertical unit. Place another washer on the end of each carriage bolt and loosely attach a wing nut to each. The diagram at right shows how the elements go together.

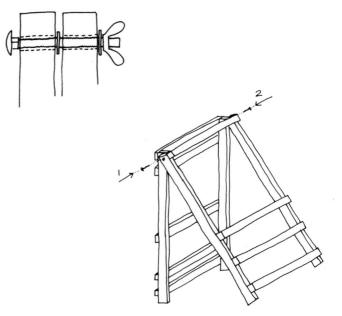

☐ Attach the vertical unit to the seat unit just as you attached the diagonal unit to the vertical unit.
☐ Tighten all four wing nuts.

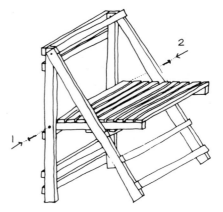

Design 2:
The C.C. Modular Seating

(A convertible seating unit/occasional table)

Materials

Wood	• One 14-foot length of 1-x-3-inch pine
	• One 8-foot length of 1-x-3-inch pine
	• Five 6-foot lengths of 1-x-2-inch pine
Hardware	• One hundred twenty-eight 4-penny finishing nails
	• Sixteen 1¼-inch wire brads
	• Four each—¼-inch by 2½-inch carriage bolts, ¼-inch washers, and ¼-inch wing nuts
	• Twelve 1½-inch flathead wood screws
Glue	• Approximately two ounces of wood glue
Sandpaper	• Two sheets of medium-grain sandpaper
	• Two sheets of fine-grain sandpaper

Step 1: Cut the wood to size.

☐ From the 1-x-3-inch stock cut nine pieces, each 25 inches long.

☐ From each of two 6-foot lengths of 1-x-2-inch stock, cut four pieces: two 24 inches long; one 12 inches long; and one 9½ inches long.

☐ From each of two 6-foot length of 1-x-2-inch stock cut four pieces: three 19 inches long and one 13 inches long.

☐ From one 6-foot length of 1-x-2-inch stock cut five pieces: two 19 inches long; two 13 inches long; and one 7 inches long.

Step 2: Sand the wood.

Step 3: Build two identical side trusses.

☐ Start two 1¼-inch wire brads into each end of two 13-inch-long pieces.

☐ Place one 24-inch-long and one 19-inch-long piece on the work surface, parallel to one another, as shown, so that the distance from the outer edge of one to the outer edge of the other is 12 inches.

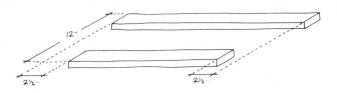

☐ Place the two 13-inch-long pieces on the 19- and 24-inch-long pieces and trace an outline of the top pieces on those below.

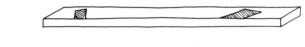

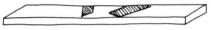

☐ Remove the 13-inch-long pieces and spread glue on the 24-inch-long and 19-inch-long pieces inside the marks.

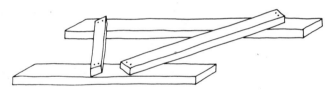

☐ Replace the 13-inch-long pieces on the glued areas and nail them into position. As you nail make sure that the pieces stay in place.

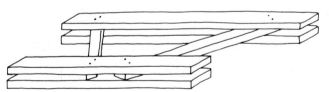

☐ Glue and nail one 19-inch-long piece and one 24-inch-long piece to the 13-inch-long pieces just above the other two using 4-penny finishing nails.

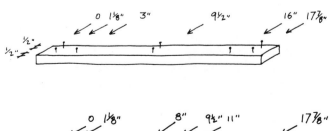

☐ Repeat all of Step 3 to create a second side truss identical to the first.

Step 4: Build the center truss.

☐ Start eight nails into one 19-inch-long piece as shown; this is one top piece of the center truss.

☐ Start eight nails into a second 19-inch-long piece as shown; this is one bottom piece of the center truss.

☐ Place two unnailed 19-inch-long pieces on the work surface parallel to one another so that the distance from the outer edge of one to the outer edge of the other is 7 inches.

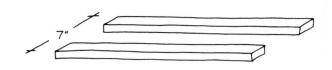

☐ Place two 12-inch-long pieces perpendicularly across the 19-inch-long pieces as shown.

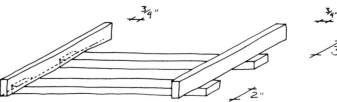

☐ Place one 7-inch and two 9½-inch-long pieces between the 12-inch-long pieces as shown. The 7-inch-long piece is centered between the 12-inch-long pieces.

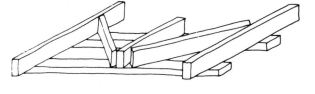

☐ Spread glue on the 12-inch-long, 9½-inch-long, and 7-inch-long pieces above the 19-inch-long pieces.

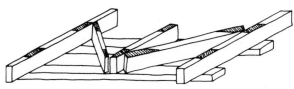

☐ Place the 19-inch-long pieces that have nails started into them across the glued surfaces positioned on top of the 12-inch, 9½-inch, and 7-inch-long pieces, just as the 19-inch-long pieces are positioned below them. Carefully nail the pieces into place.

☐ Remove the two 19-inch-long pieces from under the other pieces and start nails into them as you did into the other two 19-inch-long pieces.

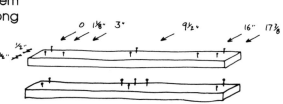

☐ Turn the assembly over and spread glue on the 12-inch, 9½-inch, and 7-inch-long pieces as before.

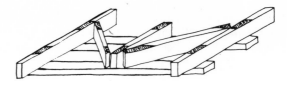

☐ Place the 19-inch-long pieces on the glued surfaces and nail them into position.

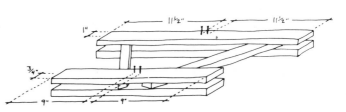

Step 5: Assemble the base.

☐ Start four nails into each of the two side trusses.

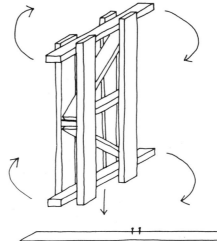

☐ Use a twisting motion to fit the center truss into one of the side trusses as shown.

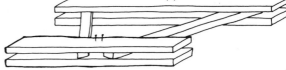

☐ Center the center truss and nail it into position.

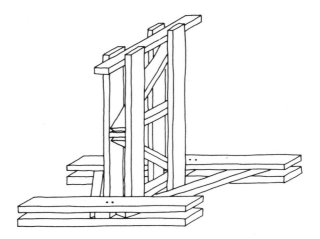

☐ Twist the other end of the center truss into the other side truss and nail it into position.

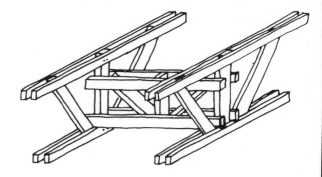

Step 6: Attach the top pieces.

☐ Glue and nail six 25-inch-long 1-x-3-inch pieces to the base as shown. The first piece overhangs the end of the top of the base by ¼ inch.

☐ Attach the remaining three 25-inch-long pieces to the base using 1½-inch flathead wood screws as shown.

Step 7: Convert to seating unit.

☐ Remove the three 25-inch-long pieces that you attached with screws.

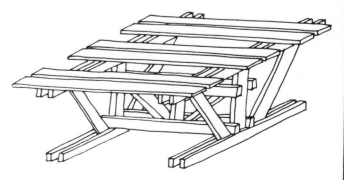

□ Drill ¼-inch holes through the protruding ends of the 24-inch-long pieces and the 19-inch-long pieces below them.

□ Slide two of the loose 25-inch-long pieces between the holes and drill holes in them.

□ Slide carriage bolts through the holes and bolt them into position.
□ Drill two holes (in addition to the holes already there) the size of your wood screws into the remaining 25-inch-long pieces.

□ Use two 1½-inch flathead wood screws to attach the piece just drilled to the upright 25-inch-long pieces.

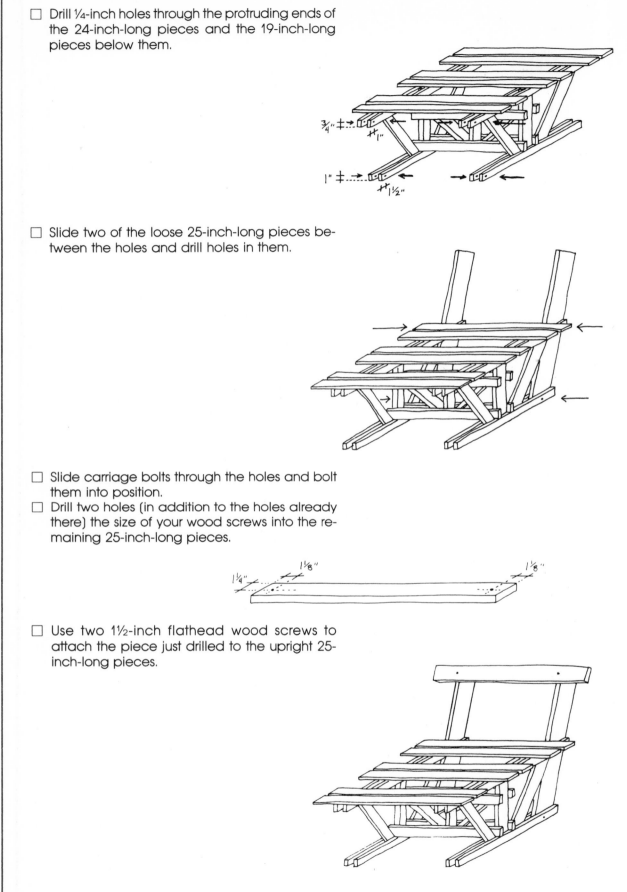

How to make the cushions for the
C. C. Modular

Materials

Foam Rubber	• One 18-x-16-x-2-inch piece, high density—for the seat cushion
	• One 18-x-14-x-2-inch piece, medium density—for the back cushion
Fiberfil	• One 25-x-74-x-2-inch piece—for the seat cushion
	• One 25-x-66-x-2-inch piece—for the back cushion
Lining Fabric	• One 29-x-48-inch piece—for the seat cushion
	• One 29-x-44-inch piece—for the back cushion
Upholstery Fabric	• One 29-x-96-inch piece

Step 1: Sew the inner envelopes.

☐ Fold the 29-by-48-inch piece of fabric in half to form a rectangle 29 inches by 24 inches. Sew two seams, as shown, to make the lining case for the seat cushion.

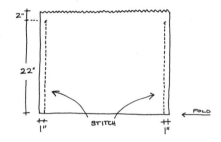

☐ Fold the 29-by-44-inch piece of fabric in half to form a rectangle 29 inches by 22 inches. Sew two seams, as shown, to make the lining case for the back cushion.

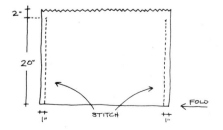

Step 2: Sew the outer envelope.

☐ Fold the upholstery fabric as shown and sew four seams. After sewing you will turn the piece inside out, so when you fold make sure that the outer surface of the fabric is face in. The cross-hatched areas on the drawing represent the outer surface of the fabric.

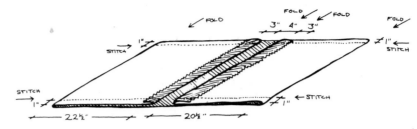

Step 3: Fill the envelopes.

☐ Wrap the 74-inch-long piece of Fiberfil twice around the 18-by-16-inch piece of foam.

☐ Turn the lining for the seat cushions rightside out (the seams will be on the inside) and stuff the Fiberfil-wrapped foam into it.

☐ Sew the 2-inch hem inside.

☐ Wrap the 66-inch-long piece of Fiberfil twice around the 18-by-14-inch piece of foam.

☐ Turn the lining for the back cushion right side out (the seam will be on the inside) and stuff the Fiberfil-wrapped foam into it.

☐ Sew the 2-inch seam inside.

☐ Turn the outer envelope rightside out (the seams will be on the inside) and stuff the appropriately sized pillows into the appropriately sized pockets.

☐ Place the cushions on the chair.

TABLES

Design 3:
The Thirty-Four-Inch-Square Adjustable-Height Table

Materials

Wood	• One 6-foot length of 1-x-2-inch pine
	• Twelve 6-foot lengths of 1-x-3-inch pine
Nails	• Ninety-six 1¼-inch wire brads
	• One hundred and eighteen 4-penny finishing nails
Bolts	• Two each—¼-inch by 2-inch carriage bolts and wing nuts and four washers
Glue	• Approximately two ounces of wood glue
Sandpaper	• Two sheets of medium-grain sandpaper
	• Two sheets of fine-grain sandpaper

Step 1: Cut wood to size.

- ☐ Cut two 1-x-2-inch pieces, 32¾ inches long each.
- ☐ Cut fourteen 1-x-3-inch pieces, 32¾ inches long each.
- ☐ Cut two 1-x-3-inch pieces, 34¼ inches long each.
- ☐ Cut four 1-x-3-inch pieces, 35⅞ inches long each.
- ☐ Cut four 1-x-3-inch pieces, 18 inches long each.
- ☐ Cut four 1-x-3-inch pieces, 16⅜ inches long each.

Step 2: Sand the wood.

Step 3: Build the table top.

- ☐ Start forty-eight 1¼-inch nails into each of the two 1-x-2-inch pieces.

- ☐ Mark four lines across twelve of the fourteen 32¾-inch-long 1-x-3-inch pieces.

- ☐ Place the twelve marked pieces on the work surface, lines facing up, parallel to one another. From the outer edge of the first to the outer edge of the last is a dimension of 32¾ inches. The spaces between the pieces are each approximately ¼ inch.

☐ Spread glue in two areas on each of the pieces as indicated by the pairs of pencil lines.

☐ One at a time, place the 1-x-2-inch pieces across the glued surfaces and nail them into place. As you nail make sure that the pieces stay square, parallel, and aligned.

26

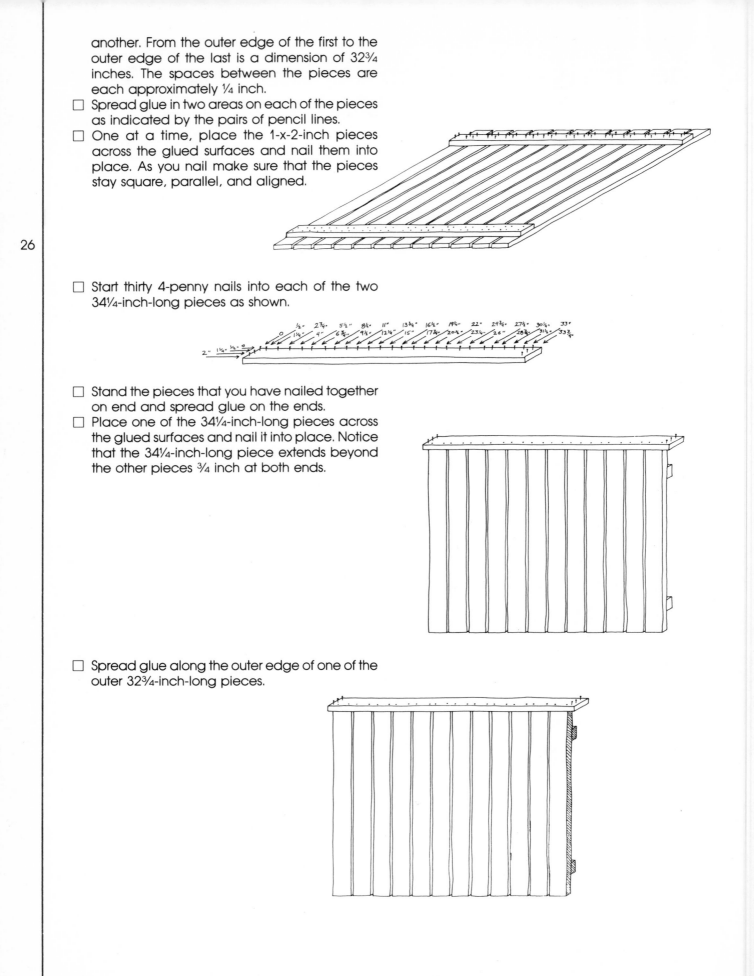

☐ Start thirty 4-penny nails into each of the two 34¼-inch-long pieces as shown.

☐ Stand the pieces that you have nailed together on end and spread glue on the ends.

☐ Place one of the 34¼-inch-long pieces across the glued surfaces and nail it into place. Notice that the 34¼-inch-long piece extends beyond the other pieces ¾ inch at both ends.

☐ Spread glue along the outer edge of one of the outer 32¾-inch-long pieces.

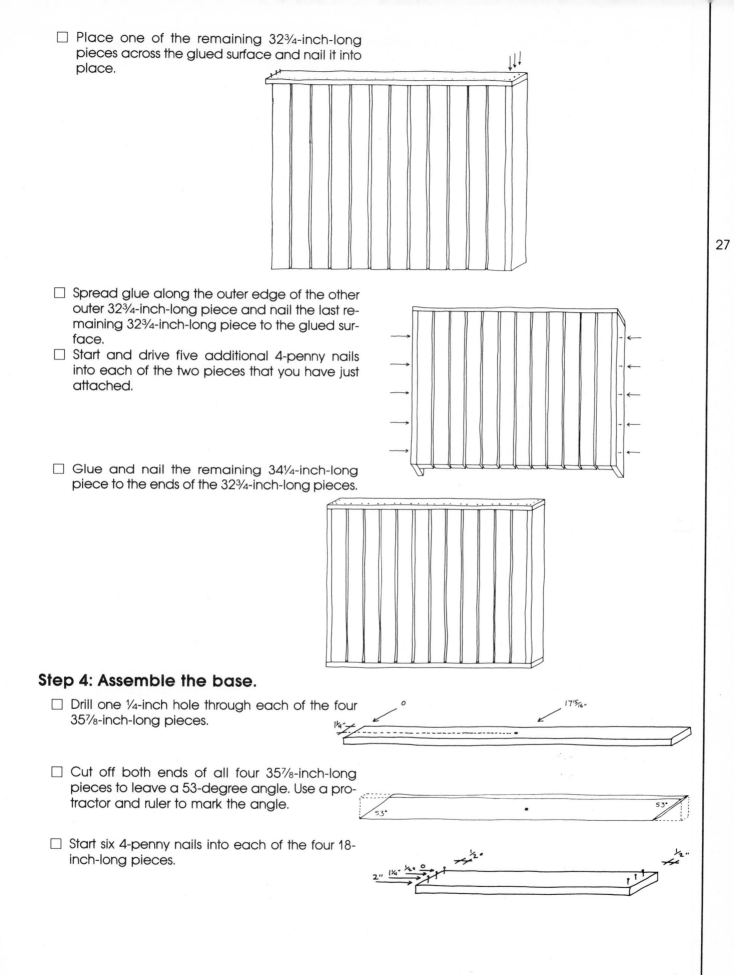

☐ Place one of the remaining 32¾-inch-long pieces across the glued surface and nail it into place.

☐ Spread glue along the outer edge of the other outer 32¾-inch-long piece and nail the last remaining 32¾-inch-long piece to the glued surface.

☐ Start and drive five additional 4-penny nails into each of the two pieces that you have just attached.

☐ Glue and nail the remaining 34¼-inch-long piece to the ends of the 32¾-inch-long pieces.

Step 4: Assemble the base.

☐ Drill one ¼-inch hole through each of the four 35⅞-inch-long pieces.

☐ Cut off both ends of all four 35⅞-inch-long pieces to leave a 53-degree angle. Use a protractor and ruler to mark the angle.

☐ Start six 4-penny nails into each of the four 18-inch-long pieces.

- [ ] Start six 4-penny nails into each of the four 16⅜-inch-long pieces.

- [ ] Mark four lines across one ¾-inch edge of each of the 35⅞-inch-long pieces.

- [ ] Mark four lines across the other ¾-inch edge of each of the 35⅞-inch-long pieces.

- [ ] Place two 35⅞-inch-long pieces on the work surface parallel to one another so that the distance from the outer edge of one to the outer edge of the other is 18 inches.
- [ ] Spread glue on both pieces between the first and second lines and between the third and fourth lines.
- [ ] One at a time nail the two 18-inch-long pieces across the glued surfaces. As you nail make sure that the pieces stay parallel, square, and aligned.
- [ ] Turn the pieces over. Glue and nail the remaining two 18-inch-long pieces to the 35⅞-inch-long pieces as indicated by the pencil lines.

- [ ] Place the remaining two 35⅞-inch-long pieces on the work surface parallel to one another so that the distance from the outer edge of one to the outer edge of the other is 16⅜ inches.
- [ ] Glue and nail the four 16⅜-inch-long pieces to the remaining 35⅞-inch-long pieces just as you nailed the 18-inch-long pieces to the other 35⅞-inch-long pieces.
- [ ] Slide the smaller base piece into the larger base piece and attach them using the carriage bolts, washers, and wing nuts.

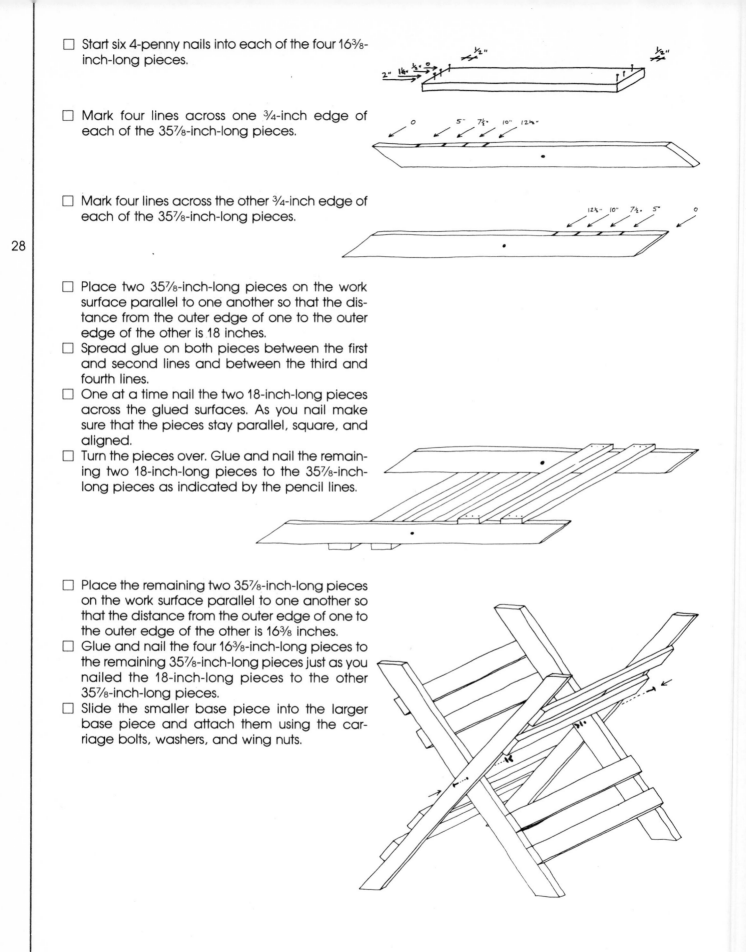

Step 5: Allow glue to dry thoroughly, for at least twelve hours.

Step 6: Apply desired finishing material.

Step 7: Place the top on the base according to the drawing for either dining/desk/game height or occasional-table height.

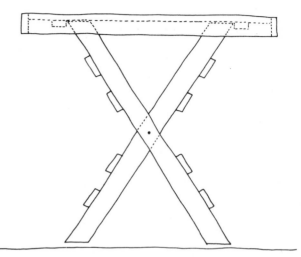

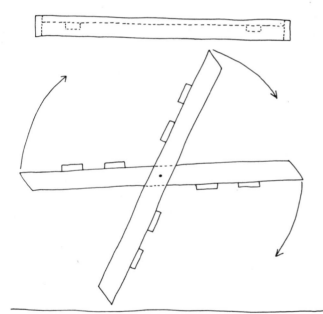

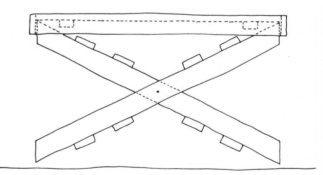

Design 4:
The Dining Table

Materials

Wood
- Fifteen 8-foot lengths of 1-x-3-inch pine
- One 6-foot length of 1-x-3-inch pine

Nails
- One hundred 4-penny finishing nails
- Two hundred and forty 1¼-inch wire brads

Bolts
- Four ¼-inch-by-2½-inch carriage bolts plus ¼-inch washers and wing nuts

Screws
- Eight 2-inch flathead wood screws

Glue
- Approximately four ounces of wood glue

Sandpaper
- Three sheets of medium-grain sandpaper
- Three sheets of fine-grain sandpaper

Step 1: Cut wood to size.

- ☐ From each of ten 8-foot lengths cut two pieces, one 68 inches long and one 26½ inches long.
- ☐ From each of two 8-foot lengths cut two pieces, one 68 inches long and one 18¾ inches long.
- ☐ From each of two 8-foot lengths cut four pieces, two 29 inches long and two 18¾ inches long.
- ☐ From one 8-foot length cut three pieces, two 32 inches long and one 29 inches long.
- ☐ From the 6-foot length cut two pieces, each 18¾ inches long.

Step 2: Sand the wood.

Step 3: Assemble two identical support frames.

- ☐ Drill two ¼-inch holes, centered as shown, in one of the 26½-inch-long pieces.

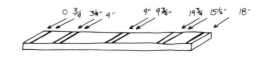

- ☐ Mark eight lines across four of the 18¾-inch-long pieces.

□ Start fifteen 4-penny nails into two of the marked pieces on the side opposite the marks.

□ Start ten 4-penny nails into the other two marked pieces on the side opposite the marks.

□ Position five 26½-inch-long pieces on the work surface. The center piece is the piece with the predrilled holes. The holes are nearer the top than the bottom.
□ Spread glue on the ¾-inch edge of each of the five 26½-inch-long pieces in an area from the bottom and up 2½ inches.
□ Place one of the 18¾-inch-long pieces that has fifteen nails started into it across the glued surfaces. Use the lines on the underside of the 18¾-inch-long piece as guides for exact placement.

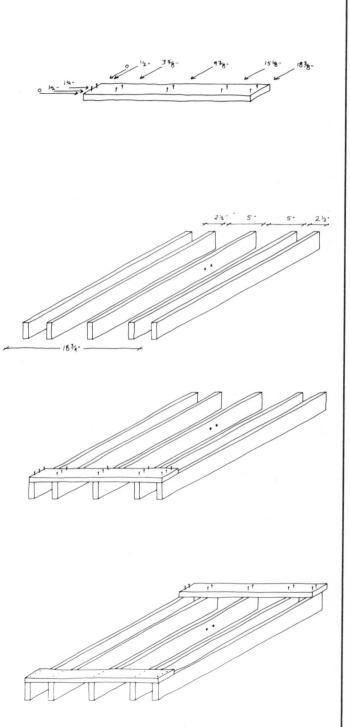

□ Nail the 18¾-inch-long piece into place as you make sure that the pieces stay square, parallel, and aligned.
□ Spread glue on the ¾-inch edge of the five 26½-inch-long pieces at the top end. The glue will cover an area on each from the top end down 1¾ inches.
□ Place one 18¾-inch-long piece that has ten nails started into it across the glued surfaces. Notice that the top edge of the 18¾-inch-long piece is ¾ inches above the top ends of the 26½-inch-long pieces and that all the nails go into the 26½-inch-long pieces. Use the lines on the underside of the 18¾-inch-long piece as guides for placement.

□ Nail the 18¾-inch-long piece into place. As you nail make sure that the pieces stay square and parallel.
□ Turn the support frame over and repeat the preceding six steps to attach two more 18¾-inch-long pieces.
□ Repeat all of Step 3 to assemble a second support frame identical to the first support frame.

Step 4: Assemble the table top.

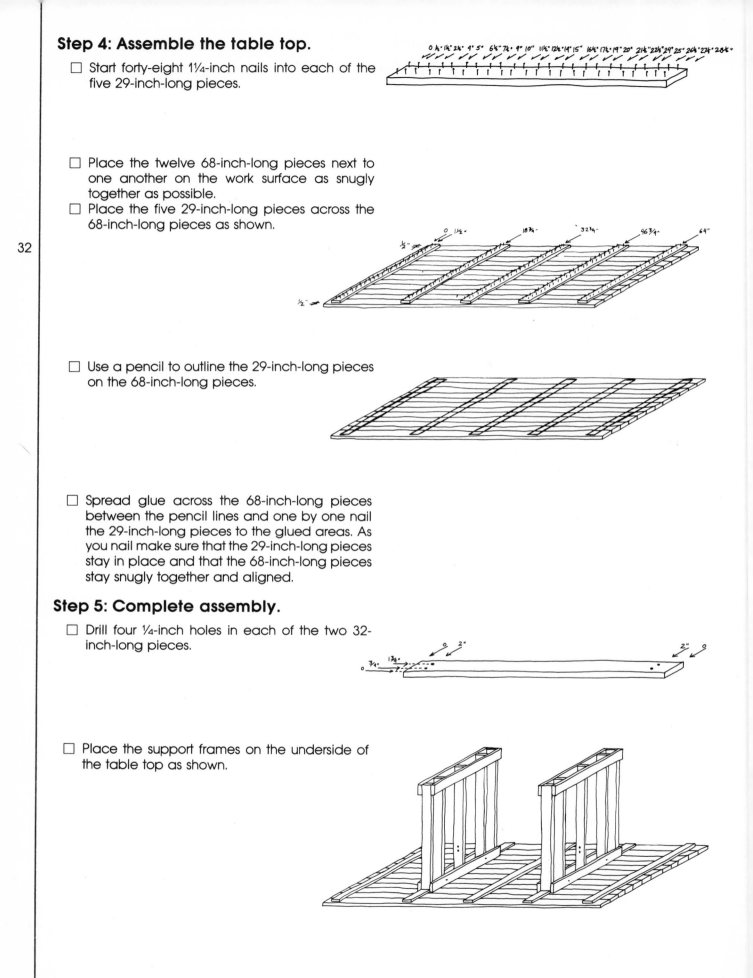

☐ Start forty-eight 1¼-inch nails into each of the five 29-inch-long pieces.

☐ Place the twelve 68-inch-long pieces next to one another on the work surface as snugly together as possible.

☐ Place the five 29-inch-long pieces across the 68-inch-long pieces as shown.

☐ Use a pencil to outline the 29-inch-long pieces on the 68-inch-long pieces.

☐ Spread glue across the 68-inch-long pieces between the pencil lines and one by one nail the 29-inch-long pieces to the glued areas. As you nail make sure that the 29-inch-long pieces stay in place and that the 68-inch-long pieces stay snugly together and aligned.

Step 5: Complete assembly.

☐ Drill four ¼-inch holes in each of the two 32-inch-long pieces.

☐ Place the support frames on the underside of the table top as shown.

32

☐ Screw four screws through each support frame into the 29-inch-long piece of the table top.

☐ Attach the 32-inch-long pieces to both sides of the center verticals of the two support frames using the four carriage bolts, washers, and wing nuts.

Step 6: Turn the table rightside up and allow the glue to dry for at least twelve hours.

Step 7: Apply finishing material as desired.

Design 5:
The Occasional Table

Materials

Wood	• Four 6-foot lengths of 1-x-3-inch pine
Nails	• One 6-foot length of 1-x-2-inch pine
	• Seventy-three 1¼-inch wire brads
Glue	• Approximately two ounces of wood glue
Sandpaper	• Two sheets of medium-grain sandpaper
	• Two sheets of fine-grain sandpaper

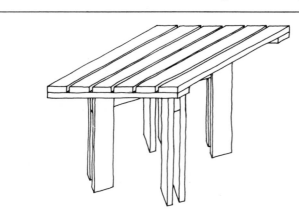

Step 1: Cut wood to size.

☐ From the 1-x-3-inch pine cut eight 16¼-inch-long pieces.

☐ From the 1-x-3-inch pine cut eight 15½-inch-long pieces.

☐ From the 1-x-2-inch pine cut two 16¼-inch-long pieces.

Step 2: Sand the wood.

Step 3: Assemble the table top.

☐ Start twelve nails into each of the two 1-x-2-inch pieces.

☐ Place six of the 16¼-inch-long 1-x-3-inch pieces on the work surface parallel to one another with spaces of approximately ¼ inch between each. The distance from the outer edge of the

first piece to the outer edge of the last should be 16¼ inches.

☐ Spread glue on both ends of each of the six pieces from the ends in 1⅝ inches.

☐ Place the 1-x-2-inch pieces across the glued surfaces and, one at a time, nail them into position. As you nail make sure that the pieces stay square, parallel and aligned.

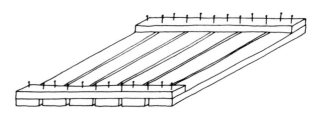

Step 4: Assemble the two sections of the base.

☐ Start four nails into each of four 15½-inch-long pieces.

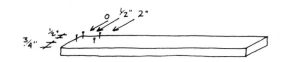

☐ Spread glue at both ends of one 16¼-inch-long 1-x-3-inch piece from the ends in 2½ inches.

☐ Nail one 15½-inch-long piece at a right angle to each 16¼-inch-long piece. As you nail make sure that the pieces stay square.

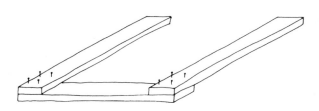

☐ Turn the pieces over, then glue and nail two more 15½-inch-long pieces to the 16¼-inch-long piece.

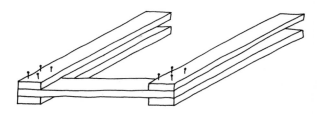

☐ Start four nails into the remaining four 15½-inch-long pieces.

☐ Spread glue at both ends of the remaining 16¼-inch-long piece from the ends in 2½ inches.

☐ Glue and nail two 15½-inch-long pieces at a right angle to the 16¼-inch-long piece so that the top end of each 15½-inch-long piece is 2½ inches above the top edge of the 16¼-inch-long piece. As you nail make sure that the pieces stay square.

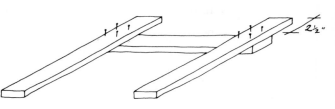

☐ Turn the pieces over to glue and nail the remaining two 15½-inch-long pieces to the other side of the 16¼-inch-long piece. As you nail make sure that the pieces stay square.

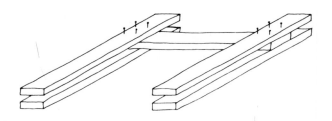

Step 5: Connect the two sections.

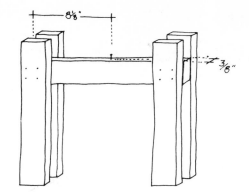

- ☐ Drive one nail ¾ inch into the center of the ¾-inch edge of the horizontal member of the second base section that you assembled.

- ☐ Use a wire cutter to snip off the head of the nail.
- ☐ Mark the center point on the underside of the horizontal member of the first base section that you assembled.

- ☐ Place that center point over the cut top of the nail in the other base section and tap it down to join the two base sections.

Step 6: Complete the assembly.

- ☐ Spread glue on the top ends of each of the eight 15½-inch-long pieces and along the top edge of the upper horizontal of the base.
- ☐ Place the top over the base and drive ten nails through the top into the base.

Step 7: Allow glue to dry thoroughly, for at least twelve hours.

Step 8: Apply finishing material as desired.

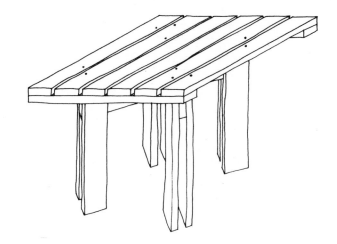

Design 6:
The Snack Table

Materials

Wood
- One 8-foot length of 1-x-2-inch pine
- Four 6-foot lengths of 1-x-2-inch pine

Nails
- Seventy-two 1¼-inch wire brads

Bolts
- Two each ¼-inch by 2-inch carriage bolts, and wing nuts, and four washers

Glue
- Approximately two ounces of wood glue

Sandpaper
- One sheet of medium-grain sandpaper
- One sheet of fine-grain sandpaper

Step 1: Cut wood to size.

☐ From each of two 6-foot lengths cut three pieces, two 28½ inches long and one 14 inches long.

☐ From each of two 6-foot lengths cut four pieces, each 17⅞ inches long.

☐ From the 8-foot length cut six pieces: two 12⅜ inches long; one 14⅜ inches long; two 15⅞ inches long; and one 17⅞ inches long.

Step 2: Sand wood.

Step 3: Build the table top.

☐ Start fourteen nails into the 14⅜-inch-long piece.

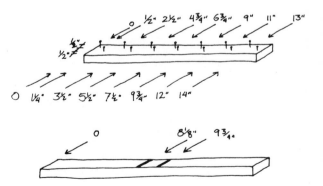

☐ Mark two lines across seven of the 17⅞-inch-long pieces.

☐ Place the seven marked 17⅞-inch-long pieces on the work surface parallel to one another and evenly spaced with the lines facing up. The distance from the outer edge of the first piece to the outer edge of the last should be 14⅜ inches; this will leave spaces between each piece of approximately ½ inch.

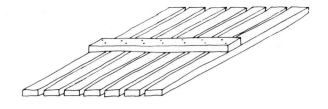

☐ Spread glue on the 17⅞-inch-long pieces between the pencil lines marked on each piece.
☐ Place the 14⅜-inch-long piece across the glued surfaces and nail it into place. As you nail make sure that the pieces stay in place, parallel, square, and aligned.

☐ Start eighteen nails into the two 15⅞-inch-long pieces.

38

☐ Stand the pieces that are nailed together on end and spread glue on the ends.
☐ Place one of the 15⅞-inch-long pieces across the glued surfaces and nail it into place. Notice that the 15⅞-inch-long piece extends beyond the outer 17⅞-inch-long pieces ¾ inch.

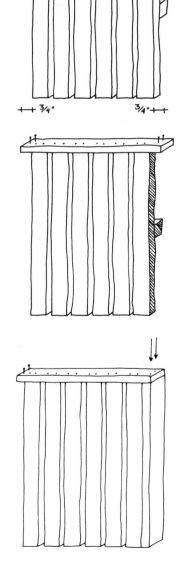

☐ Spread glue along the outer edge of one of the outer 17⅞-inch-long pieces.

☐ Place one of the remaining 17⅞-inch-long pieces against the glued surface and nail it into place.

☐ Spread glue along the outer edge of the other outer 17⅞-inch-long piece and nail the last remaining 17⅞-inch-long piece to the glued surface.

☐ Drive three nails into each of the two 17⅞-inch-long pieces that you have just attached to secure them into place.

☐ Glue and nail the remaining 15⅞-inch-long piece to the ends of the 17⅞-inch-long pieces.

Step 4: Assemble the base.

☐ Drill a ¼-inch hole through each of the four 28½-inch-long pieces.

☐ Cut off both ends of all four 28½-inch-long pieces to leave a 63-degree angle.

☐ Start four nails into each of the 14-inch-long pieces and 12⅜-inch-long pieces.

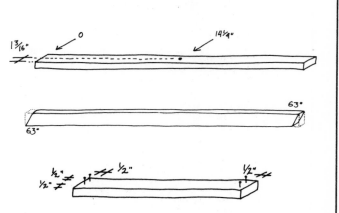

☐ Mark two lines across one ¾-inch edge of each of the 28½-inch-long pieces.

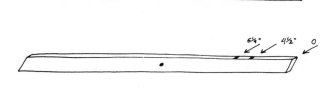

☐ Mark two lines across the other ¾-inch edge of each of the 28½-inch-long pieces.

40

☐ Place two 28½-inch-long pieces on the work surface parallel to one another so that the distance from the outer edge of one to the outer edge of the other is 14 inches.

☐ Spread glue on both pieces between the pencil lines.

☐ Nail a 14-inch-long piece across the glued surfaces. As you nail make sure that the pieces stay parallel, square, and aligned.

☐ Turn the pieces over. Glue and nail the other 14-inch-long piece between the pencil lines.

☐ Place the remaining two 28½-inch-long pieces on the work surface parallel to one another so that the distance from the outer edge of one to the outer edge of the other is 12⅜ inches.

☐ Glue and nail the two 12⅜-inch-long pieces to the remaining 28½-inch-long pieces just as you nailed the 14-inch-long pieces to the other 28½-inch-long pieces.

☐ Slide the smaller base piece into the larger base piece and attach the two using carriage bolts, washers, and wing nuts.

Step 5: Allow the glue to dry thoroughly, for at least twelve hours.

Step 6: Apply the desired finishing material.

Step 7: Place top on base.

BED

Design 7:
The Four Poster Bed

NOTE: This project contains almost two hundred pieces. It is clearly the most ambitious project in this book. Before you start it, you should "practice" with a few simpler designs. Also, if you plan to conquer this project you have become a fairly serious carpenter and, if you don't already own one, this may be the time to invest in a table saw.

Materials

Wood	• Twenty-two 14-foot lengths of 1-x-3-inch pine
	• Twenty-seven 10-foot lengths of 1-x-3-inch pine
	• One 6-foot length of 1-x-3-inch pine
Nails	• Two and one quarter pounds of 4-penny finishing nails
Bolts	• Sixteen each of ¼-inch by 4½-inch carriage bolts, ¼-inch washers, and ¼-inch wing nuts.
	• Sixteen each of ¼-inch by 3½-inch carriage bolts, ¼-inch washers, and ¼-inch wing nuts
Glue	• Approximately twenty-four ounces of wood glue
Sandpaper	• Eight sheets of medium-grain sandpaper
	• Eight sheets of fine-grain sandpaper

Step 1: Cut wood to size.

- ☐ From each of four 14-foot lengths cut two 83-inch-long pieces.
- ☐ From each of six 14-foot lengths cut two 81-inch-long pieces.
- ☐ From each of seven 14-foot lengths cut two 49½-inch-long pieces and two 32-inch-long pieces.
- ☐ From each of four 14-foot lengths cut twelve 13½-inch-long pieces.
- ☐ From one 14-foot length cut two 76-inch-long pieces.

- ☐ From each of four 10-foot lengths cut two 53-inch-long pieces.
- ☐ From one 10-foot length cut two 46-inch-long pieces.
- ☐ From each of twenty-two 10-foot lengths cut two 52½-inch-long pieces.
- ☐ Cut sixty-six 6¾-inch-long pieces from the 6-foot length and the leftover pieces.

Step 2: Sand wood.

Step 3: Assemble two identical side boards.

- ☐ Mark forty-four lines across four of the 81-inch-long pieces.

- ☐ Start sixty-six nails into two of the marked 81-inch-long pieces on the side opposite the markings.

- ☐ Place twenty-two 13½-inch-long pieces on the work surface on one ¾-inch edge parallel to one another. The distance from the outer edge of the first to the outer edge of the last is 69 inches; this leaves a space of 2½ inches between each piece. Use the marks on the unnailed 81-inch-long pieces as positioning guides for the 13½-inch-long pieces.

- ☐ Spread glue on each of the 13½-inch-long pieces from the bottom end up 2½ inches.

☐ Place one of the 81-inch-long pieces that has nails started into it across the glued surface and nail it into place. Use the lines on the underside as guides for exact positioning. As you nail make sure that the pieces stay square, parallel, and aligned.

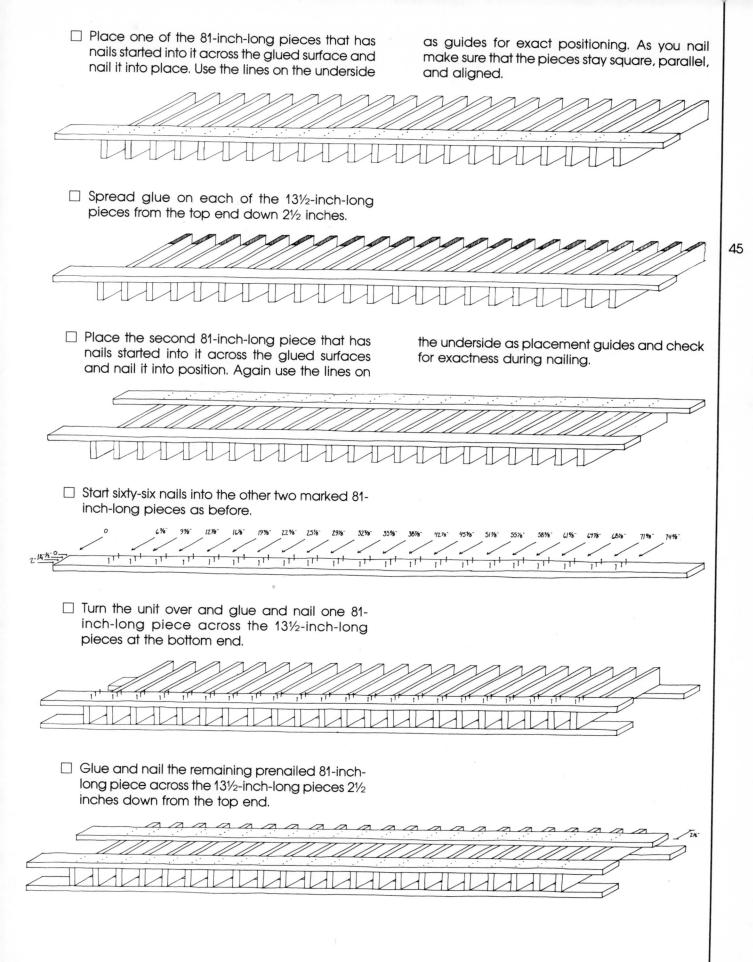

☐ Spread glue on each of the 13½-inch-long pieces from the top end down 2½ inches.

☐ Place the second 81-inch-long piece that has nails started into it across the glued surfaces and nail it into position. Again use the lines on the underside as placement guides and check for exactness during nailing.

☐ Start sixty-six nails into the other two marked 81-inch-long pieces as before.

☐ Turn the unit over and glue and nail one 81-inch-long piece across the 13½-inch-long pieces at the bottom end.

☐ Glue and nail the remaining prenailed 81-inch-long piece across the 13½-inch-long pieces 2½ inches down from the top end.

☐ Repeat all of Step 3 to assemble a second side board that is identical to the first.

Step 4: Assemble the footboard.

☐ Mark thirty-four lines across three of the 53-inch-long pieces.

☐ Mark six lines across one 53-inch-long piece.

☐ Mark twenty-eight lines across one 46-inch-long piece.

☐ Start fifty-four nails into each of the 53-inch-long pieces that have thirty-four lines marked on them. Start the nails on the side opposite the lines.

☐ Start twelve nails into the 53-inch-long piece that has six lines marked across it. Start the nails on the side opposite the lines.

☐ Start forty-two nails into the 46-inch-long piece on the side opposite the lines.

☐ Mark five lines across one ¾-inch edge of four 83-inch-long pieces.

0   4"   6½"   32½"   36"   2½"   0

☐ Position the fourteen 32-inch-long pieces on the work surface parallel to one another as shown. The distance from the outer edge of the first to the outer edge of the last is 43 inches; there are 2½-inch spaces between each piece.

43"

2½" 2½" 2½" 2½" 2½" 2½" 2½" 2½" 2½" 2½" 2½" 2½" 2½"

☐ Position the four marked 83-inch-long pieces parallel to the 32-inch-long pieces, two on each side. The bottom line on each of the 83-inch-long pieces is even with the bottom end of the 32-inch-long pieces; there is a 1-inch space between the two pieces at each side and a space of 2½ inches between the inner 83-inch-long pieces and the outer 32-inch-long pieces.

53"

2½"   2½"

☐ Spread glue in three areas, as defined by the pencil marks on each of the four 83-inch-long pieces. Also spread glue in two areas on each of the fourteen 32-inch-long pieces from the bottom up 2½ inches and from the top down 2½ inches.

☐ Nail three 53-inch-long pieces across the glued surfaces. The center piece and the lower piece each have fifty-four started nails. The upper piece has twelve started nails. Use the lines on the underside of the 53-inch-long pieces as placement guides. As you nail make sure that the pieces stay square, parallel, and aligned.

☐ Turn the unit over and glue and nail the remaining 53-inch-long piece, which has fifty-four started nails, to the unit. This piece goes directly opposite the middle piece on the other side. Use the lines on the underside as placement guides.

☐ Glue and nail the 46-inch-long piece to the bottom of the 32-inch-long pieces. Use the lines on the underside as placement guides.

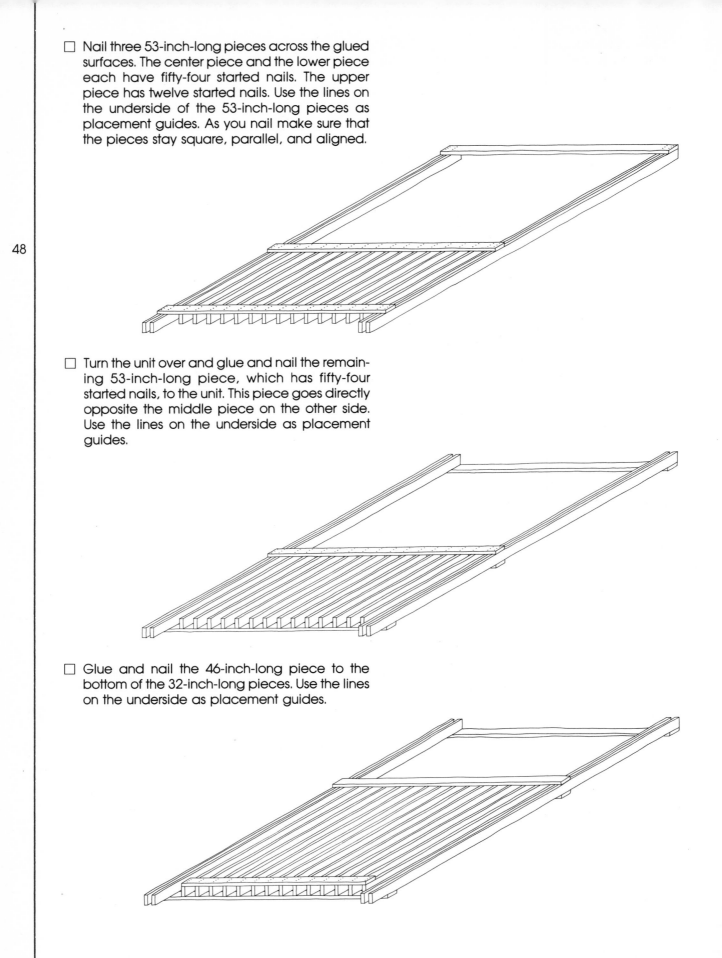

☐ Glue and nail two 13½-inch-long pieces, one at each side, to the 83-inch-long pieces. The pieces are 4 inches up from the bottom.

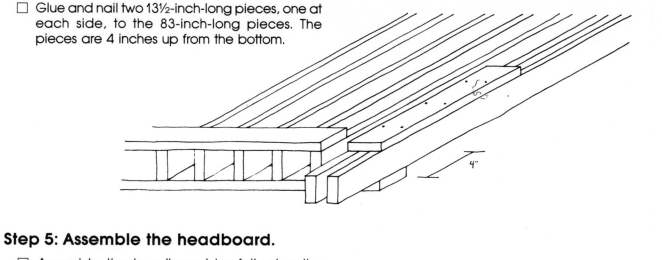

Step 5: Assemble the headboard.

☐ Assemble the headboard by following the same procedure which you used to assemble the footboard, with two differences: (1) Use fourteen 49½-inch-long pieces instead of the fourteen 32-inch-long pieces; (2) Mark the five lines across one ¾-inch edge of the four 83-inch-long pieces as shown here rather than as shown in Step 4.

Step 6: Assemble two identical top spanners.

☐ Draw two lines across one side of each of the remaining four 81-inch-long pieces.

☐ Start ten nails into each of the four 81-inch-long pieces on the side opposite the lines.

☐ Spread glue along one ¾-inch edge of one of the 76-inch-long pieces.

☐ Nail an 81-inch-long piece across the glued surface. The 81-inch-long piece overhangs the 76-inch-long piece by 2½ inches at both ends. Use the lines on the underside of the 81-inch-long piece as placement guides.

☐ Turn the unit over and glue and nail a second 81-inch-long piece to the 76-inch-long piece as before.

☐ Repeat the preceding three substeps to assemble a second top spanner identical to the first.

Step 7: Assemble the support bars.

☐ Mark six lines across each of the forty-four 52½-inch-long pieces.

0   5"   9¾"   22⅛"   29⅝"   42¾"   49½"

☐ Start nine nails into each of the forty-four 52½-inch-long pieces on the side opposite the lines.

0   ½"   ½"·0

☐ Position three 6¾-inch-long pieces on the work surface as shown.

13⅛"   13⅛"

46½"

☐ Spread glue on the three 6¾-inch-long pieces.

☐ Place one of the 52½-inch-long pieces across the glued surfaces and nail it into place. Use the lines on the underside of the 52½-inch-long piece as placement guides.

☐ Turn the unit over and glue and nail a second 52½-inch-long piece to the other side.

☐ Repeat the preceding four substeps another twenty-one times to assemble the remaining twenty-one support bars.

Step 8: Drill holes.

☐ Drill two ¼-inch holes in each end of each of the four 81-inch-long pieces on both side-boards.

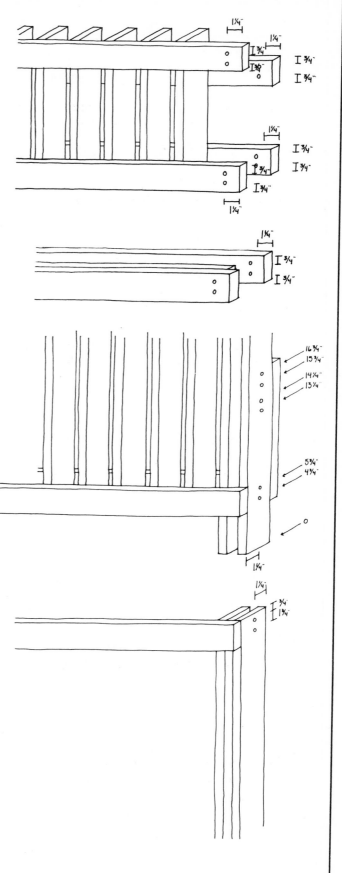

☐ Drill two ¼-inch holes in each end of each of the 81-inch-long pieces of the top spanners.

☐ Drill six ⅜-inch holes in each of the 83-inch-long pieces of the headboard and footboard near the bottom as shown.

☐ Drill two more ⅜-inch holes in each of the 83-inch-long pieces of the headboard and footboard as shown.

Step 9: Final assembly.

☐ Slide the sideboards and top spanners onto the headboard and footboard. Attach them using the carriage bolts, washers, and wing nuts. The 4½-inch-long bolts are used in the top two and bottom two holes at each corner. The 3½-inch bolts are used in the center four holes at each corner.

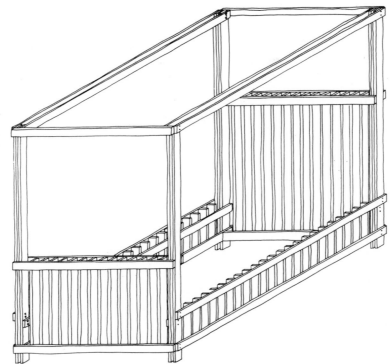

☐ Slip the support bars onto the verticals of the sideboards.

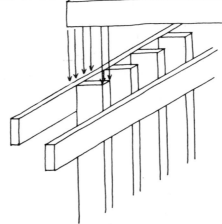

Step 10: Allow the glue to dry thoroughly, for at least twelve hours.

Step 11: Apply the desired finishing material.

Design 1   The Folding Chair

Design 2   The C.C. Modular Seating

Design 3   The Thirty-Four-Inch-Square
Adjustable-Height Table

Design 4   The Dining Table

Design 6   The Occasional Table

Design 5   The Snack Table

Design 7   The Four-Poster Bed

Design 8   The Free-Standing Shelves

Design 9   The Small Wall Unit

Buffet using the tall storage column and two small storage columns

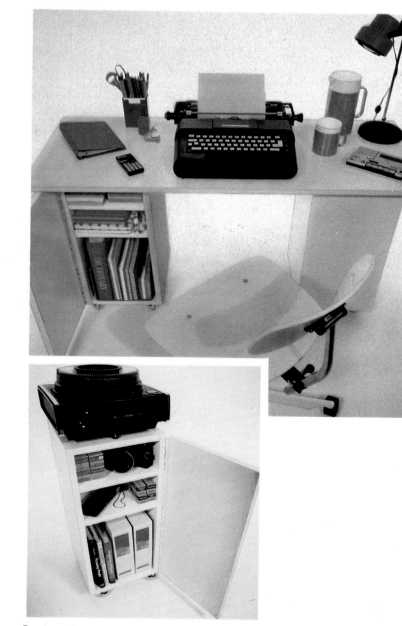

Design 11   The Tall Storage Column

Design 10   The Small Storage Column

Design 12   The Eighteen-Inch Towel Bar

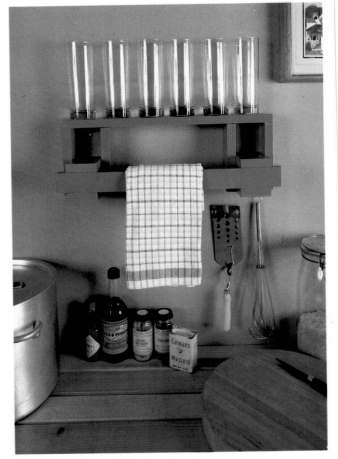

Design 14   The Thirty-Six-Inch Towel Bar

Design 13   The Twenty-Four-Inch Towel Bar

Design 15   Wall Hooks

Design 17   The Wine Rack

Design 16   The Letter Holder

Design 19   The Dressing Screen

Design 20   The Plant Box

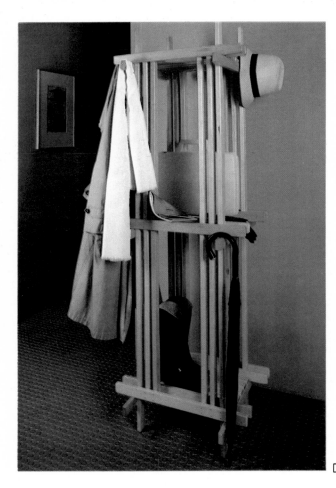

Design 18   The Coat Stand

STORAGE

Design 8:
The Free-Standing Shelves

Materials

Wood	• Twenty-one 8-foot lengths of 1-x-2-inch pine
	• Twenty 6-foot lengths of 1-x-2-inch pine
Nails	• Two-hundred and forty 4-penny finishing nails
	• Eighteen 1¼-inch wire brads
Glue	• Approximately six ounces of wood glue
Sandpaper	• Four sheets of medium-grain sandpaper
	• Four sheets of fine-grain sandpaper
Dowels	• Four 2-inch-long ⅜-inch diameter dowels to secure two stacked units (optional)

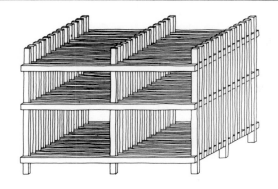

Step 1: Cut wood to size.

☐ From each of the twenty-one 8-foot lengths cut two pieces, each 47½ inches long.

☐ From each of fifteen 6-foot lengths cut two pieces, each 32½ inches long.

☐ From the remaining five 6-foot lengths cut nine pieces, each 35½ inches long.

Step 2: Sand wood.

Step 3: Build the first layer.

☐ Mark one line in the center of each of the forty-two 47½-inch-long pieces, 23¾ inches from one end as shown.

☐ Mark three lines across three of the nine 35½-inch-long pieces. (You will position the rest of the vertical pieces by lining them up with these three and squaring them with the first layer.)

↑ 0   ↑ 23¾"

← 0

← 4³⁄₁₆"

← 15⅝"

← 30¹³⁄₁₆"

☐ Line up the three horizontal (47½-inch) pieces using two marked 35½-inch-long pieces as follows: place two marked 35½-inch-long pieces parallel to one another on the work surface 47½ inches apart lines facing up. Align three 47½-inch-long pieces between the two 35½-inch-long pieces so that the top edge of each is even with one line on the 35½-inch-long pieces.

☐ Next take these two 35½-inch-long pieces, plus the third marked one, and start six 1¼-inch nails into each, two below each line marked on the wood as shown.

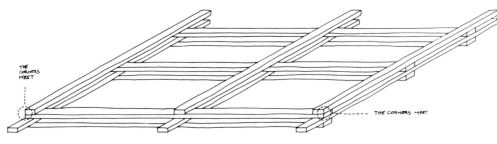

☐ Place the three 35½-inch-long pieces on top of the three 47½-inch-long pieces as shown, lining up the left edge of the center 35½-inch-long piece with the center mark on the 47½-inch-long piece.

☐ Spread glue on the 47½-inch-long pieces under the 35½-inch-long pieces.

☐ Constantly checking to make sure that the unit is square and in alignment, nail the 35½-inch-long pieces into place.

Step 4: Build ensuing layers.

☐ To build the next layer, take three more 47½-inch-long pieces (horizontals) and start six 1½-inch-long nails into each, two nails within 1½ inches of each end and two more to the right of the center mark within 1½ inches of the center mark.

☐ Spread glue on the first layer of 35½-inch-long pieces just above the first layer of 47½-inch-long pieces (horizontals).

☐ Position the next three horizontal (47½-inch-long) pieces on the glued surfaces, directly over the first set of horizontals. Use a carpenter's square for alignment.

☐ Nail the horizontals into place, constantly checking to be sure that the unit is square.

☐ Take three 32½-inch-long (short vertical) pieces and start six 4-penny nails into each, two at each of the three points where the horizontals cross the verticals.

☐ Glue and nail the short verticals into place, making sure that the corners meet as shown.

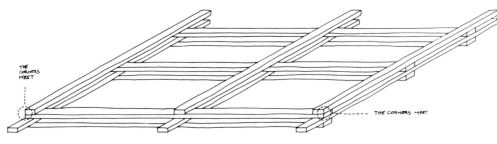

☐ Continue layering using the 47½-inch-long pieces and 32½-inch-long pieces until there are seven layers of horizontal pieces as shown.

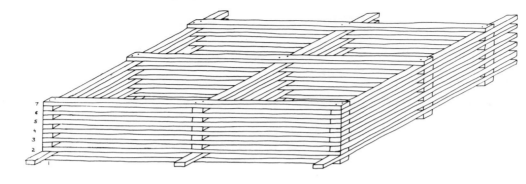

☐ For the seventh vertical layer, use three of the 35½-inch-long pieces. With a carpenter's square make sure that the bottoms of the first and seventh layer of verticals are even.

☐ Continue layering until you have glued and nailed the last set of 32½-inch-long pieces into position. There are just two more layers of horizontals and one of long verticals to be attached.

☐ Glue and nail three of the six remaining horizontal pieces into position. Then glue and nail the final layer of verticals using the three remaining 35½-inch-long pieces. With a carpenter's square align the bottoms of these verticals with the other two layers of long vertical supports.

☐ Glue and nail the final three horizontal pieces into place.

☐ Gently stand the unit up. If it is a bit wobbly the legs are uneven. Locate the long leg (or legs) causing the imbalance and sand or cut it (or them) down until the unit sits flat.

☐ Do not move the unit around until the glue has dried overnight.

Step 5: How to stack two units.

☐ If you wish to stack two units, drill one ⅜-inch hole 1 inch deep in the center of the top of each of the four corner posts of one unit and in the center of the bottom of each corner post of the other.

☐ Place a 2-inch-long by ⅜-inch-diameter dowel in the holes to keep the units steady.

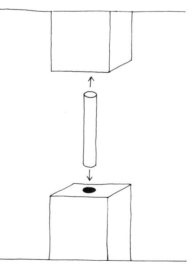

Design 9:
The Small Wall Unit

Materials

Wood	• Four 6-foot lengths of 1-x-2-inch pine
	• One 8-foot length of 1-x-2-inch pine
	• One 6-foot length of 1-x-4-inch pine
Nails	• Seventy-six 4-penny finishing nails
Screws	• Two 5-inch-long screws (for wall mounting)
Glue	• Approximately two ounces of wood glue
Sandpaper	• One sheet of medium-grain sandpaper
	• One sheet of fine-grain sandpaper

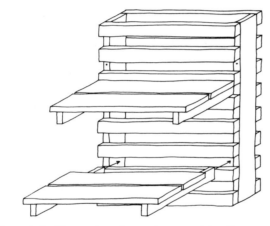

Each additional shelf requires two pieces of 1-x-2-inch pine 10⅜ inches long each, two pieces of 1-x-4-inch pine 17¾ inches long each, and eight 4-penny finishing nails.

Step 1: Cut the wood to size.

The exact width of 1-x-2-inch pine frequently varies from the ideal 1⅝ inches. When purchasing 1 x 2s for this project, make sure that the boards are all consistent in width. If the width of your 1 x 2s is not precisely 1⅝ inches, you will have to vary some of the dimensions listed for this project. To calculate the exact length for the vertical pieces of the wall bracket, multiply the precise width of your 1 x 2s by 15. When assembling the wall bracket, substitute the precise width of your 1 x 2s for the dimension 1⅝ inches whenever it appears.

☐ From each of the four 6-foot lengths of 1-x-2 pine cut four pieces, each 17¾ inches long.
☐ From the 8-foot length of 1-x-2-inch pine cut six pieces, two 24⅜ inches long and four 10⅜ inches long (see directions for calculating exact lengths at the beginning of this step).
☐ From the 6-foot length of 1-x-4 inch pine cut four pieces, each 17¾ inches long.

Step 2: Sand the wood.

Step 3: Assemble the wall bracket.

☐ Use a pencil to lightly mark fourteen lines across both ¾-inch edges of both 24⅜-inch-long pieces.

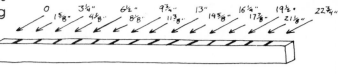

☐ Start four nails into each of the sixteen 17¾-inch-long pieces.

☐ Position the two 24⅜-inch-long pieces on the work surface parallel to one another so that the distance from the outer edge of one to the outer edge of the other is 17¾ inches.

☐ Spread glue on both 24⅜-inch-long pieces between the bottom end and the first line.

☐ Place one 17¾-inch-long piece across the glued surfaces and nail it into position. As you nail make sure that the pieces stay square, parallel, and aligned.

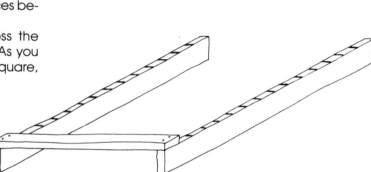

☐ Spread glue on both 24⅜-inch-long pieces between the top end and the last pencil line.

☐ Place one 17¾-inch-long piece across the glued surfaces and nail it into position. As you nail make sure that the pieces stay square and parallel.

☐ Glue and nail six more 17¾-inch-long pieces to the 24⅜-inch-long pieces, evenly spaced between the first two, according to the pencil lines.

☐ Turn the unit over and glue and nail eight more 17¾-inch-long pieces to the other side according to the lines.

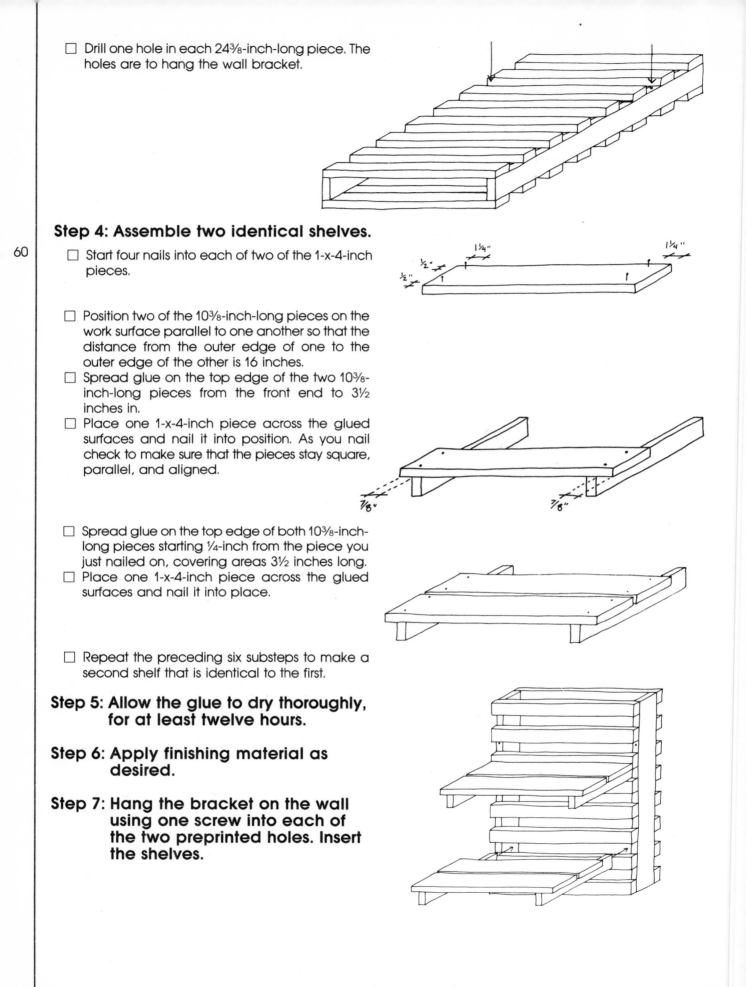

☐ Drill one hole in each 24⅜-inch-long piece. The holes are to hang the wall bracket.

Step 4: Assemble two identical shelves.

☐ Start four nails into each of two of the 1-x-4-inch pieces.

☐ Position two of the 10⅜-inch-long pieces on the work surface parallel to one another so that the distance from the outer edge of one to the outer edge of the other is 16 inches.

☐ Spread glue on the top edge of the two 10⅜-inch-long pieces from the front end to 3½ inches in.

☐ Place one 1-x-4-inch piece across the glued surfaces and nail it into position. As you nail check to make sure that the pieces stay square, parallel, and aligned.

☐ Spread glue on the top edge of both 10⅜-inch-long pieces starting ¼-inch from the piece you just nailed on, covering areas 3½ inches long.

☐ Place one 1-x-4-inch piece across the glued surfaces and nail it into place.

☐ Repeat the preceding six substeps to make a second shelf that is identical to the first.

Step 5: Allow the glue to dry thoroughly, for at least twelve hours.

Step 6: Apply finishing material as desired.

Step 7: Hang the bracket on the wall using one screw into each of the two preprinted holes. Insert the shelves.

Design 10:
The Small Storage Column

Materials

Wood	• Two 6-foot lengths of 1-x-12-inch pine
Hardware	• Two ounces of 4-penny finishing nails
	• One 23½-inch-long piano hinge
	• Twenty-five ⅝-inch flathead wood screws
Glue	• Two ounces of wood glue
Sandpaper	• One sheet of medium-grain sandpaper
	• One sheet of fine-grain sandpaper

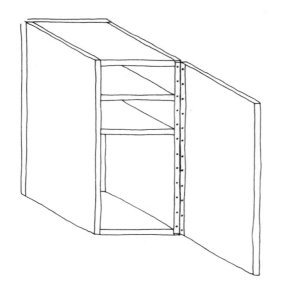

Step 1: Cut wood to size.

☐ Cut one 6-foot length into three 24-inch-long pieces, one for the back and two for the sides.

☐ Cut the other 6-foot length into one 23½-inch door and four pieces for column top, bottom, and two shelves. (Remember that a piece of 1-x-12-inch pine will measure about ¾ inch by 11¼ inch, depending on the lumberyard that mills it.) To find the length for four pieces measure the width of your 1 x 12 and subtract 1½ inches. If your 1 x 12 is exactly 11¼ inches wide, the four pieces will each be 9¾ inches long.

Step 2: Sand the wood.

Step 3: Assemble the column.

☐ Mark lines across the two side pieces and the back piece to show where the top, bottom, and two shelves will go. The lines for the shelves are ¾ inch apart. (The marked side of the wood will be on the inside, so if one side is less visually appealing, mark on it.)

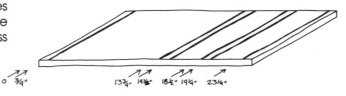

☐ Turn the pieces over. Start four rows of four nails per row: one row is ½ inch from the top end and one row is ½ inch from the bottom end securing the top and bottom while the two other rows are at the points shown to secure the shelves.

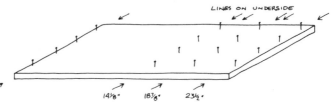

☐ Take the back piece and start ten nails, five along each side, ⅜ inch from the edge. Space these nails 5 inches apart, starting 2 inches from the top. These nails will secure the back to the side pieces.

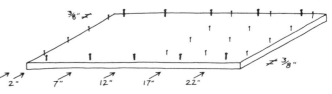

☐ Run a line of glue along one ¾-inch by 24-inch edge of one side wall and nail the back piece to the glued surface.
☐ Repeat to attach the other side wall.
☐ Take the top piece and run glue along the two 9¾-inch sides and one 11¼-inch side.
☐ Using the lines as a guide, slip the top piece into place and nail it into position.
☐ Repeat the previous two steps to attach the two shelves and the bottom piece.
☐ Place the piano hinge on the ¾-inch edge of the side wall from which the door will open. (If you're making two columns for a buffet or desk, you may want the doors to open in opposite directions—both away from the center.) The hinge should be ¼ inch short of the top and bottom of the column. Fasten with approximately twelve flathead wood screws.

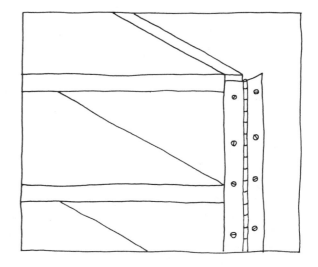

☐ Screw the hinge to the inside of the door (hinge and door should be exactly the same length) as shown in the lead diagram.

The Top for the Desk

Materials

Wood	• One 8-foot length of 1-x-10-inch pine
	• One 4-foot length of 1-x-2-inch pine
Nails	• One half ounce of 1¼-inch wire brads
Glue	• One ounce of wood glue
Sandpaper	• One sheet of medium-grain sandpaper
	• One sheet of fine-grain sandpaper

Step 1: Cut the wood to size.

☐ Cut the 8-foot length of 1-x-10-inch pine into two 48-inch-long pieces.
☐ Cut the 1 x 2 into three 16-inch-long pieces.

Step 2: Sand the wood.

Step 3: Assemble desk top.

☐ Start six nails into each of the 1-x-2-inch pieces evenly spaced.
☐ Place the two 1-x-10-inch pieces next to one another on the work surface and glue and nail one 1 x 2 across each end and the other in the center to attach the two 1-x-10-inch pieces. Each end of the 1-x-2-inch pieces will be about 1½ inches short of the edges of the 1-x-10-inch pieces.

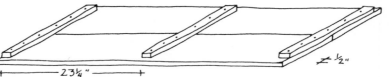

Step 4: Assemble the desk.

☐ Turn the desk top over and position it on the two 24-inch columns. The sides of the desk top will overhang 3 inches on each side and the front should be 3 inches over the front door of the column.
☐ Use 1¼-inch wire brads and glue to attach the top to the columns.
☐ To make the desk mobile, attach four 2-inch casters to each storage column.

Design 11:
The Tall Storage Column

Materials

Wood	• Six 6-foot lengths of 1-x-12-inch pine
Hardware	• Six ounces of 4-penny finishing nails
	• One 71½-inch-long piano hinge
	• Seventy-two ⅝-inch flathead wood screws
Glue	• Four ounces of wood glue
Sandpaper	• One sheet of medium-grain sandpaper
	• One sheet of fine-grain sandpaper

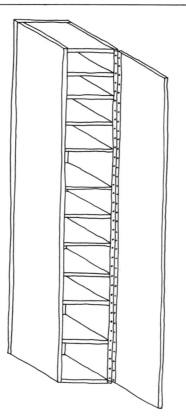

Step 1: Cut the wood to size.

☐ Three of the 6-foot 1-x-12-inch pieces make up the two sides and the back.

☐ Cut ½ inch off the fourth 1 x 12 to make a 71½-inch door.

☐ From the remaining two 1-x-12-inch pieces cut twelve pieces for the top, bottom, and ten shelves. These pieces will be approximately 9¾ inches long, but see Step 1 of "Design 10: The Small Storage Column" to find instructions for calculating the exact length.

Step 2: Sand the wood.

Step 3: Assemble the column.

☐ Mark lines as shown across the side and back pieces to indicate where the top, bottom, and ten shelves will go (or adjust the scheme shown to fit specific items that you may need to store). The space between the shelf lines is ¾ inch.

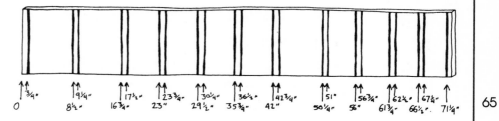

☐ Turn the pieces over and start twelve rows of nails, four nails per row, spaced as in building the 24-inch column.

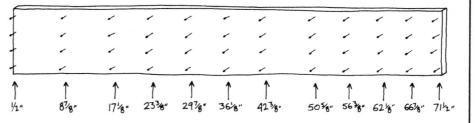

☐ Start twelve more nails into each side of the back piece, ⅜ inch in from the edge, as in building the 24-inch column. The top and bottom nails should be 2 inches from the ends and the other nails evenly spaced a little less than 7 inches apart.

☐ Follow the rest of the instructions for the 24-inch column to complete this 72-inch column.

Design 12:
The Eighteen-Inch Towel Bar/Shelf

Materials

Wood	• One 18-inch length of 1-x-2-inch pine
	• One 6-foot length of 1-x-3-inch pine
Nails	• Thirty-six 4-penny finishing nails
Screws	• Two screws for wall attachment
Glue	• Less than one ounce of wood glue
Sandpaper	• One sheet medium-grain sandpaper
	• One sheet fine-grain sandpaper

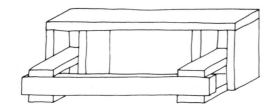

Step 1: Cut wood to size.

☐ One piece of 1-x-2-inch pine 18 inches long.
☐ From the 6-foot length of 1-x-3 pine cut one piece 18 inches long, six pieces 6 inches long, and four pieces 4 inches long.

Step 2: Sand wood.

Step 3: Assemble wall mounts.

☐ Start three nails into each of four 6-inch-long pieces.

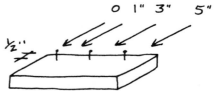

☐ Spread glue along one ¾-inch edge of one of the unnailed 6-inch-long pieces.
☐ Place one prenailed 6-inch-long piece on the glued surface and nail it into position.

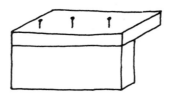

☐ Turn the unit over, placing the piece just nailed on the work surface. Spread glue on the exposed ¾-inch edge.
☐ Place a second prenailed 6-inch-long piece on the glued edge and nail it into position.

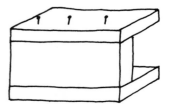

☐ Drill one hole into the center 6-inch-long piece large enough to accommodate one of the screws you have chosen to fasten the unit to the wall.

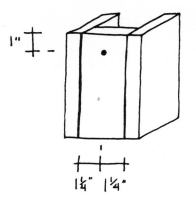

☐ Repeat the preceding six substeps to assemble a second wall mount identical to the first.

Step 4: Attach bar holders.

☐ Start two nails into two of the four 4-inch-long pieces.

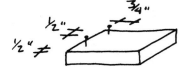

☐ Spread glue inside one wall mount at the bottom edge, as shown.
☐ Slip one of the unnailed 4-inch-long pieces into place as shown.

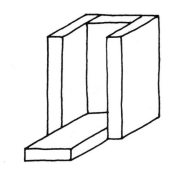

☐ Turn the wall mount onto its side and drive two nails through it into the 4-inch-long bar holder.

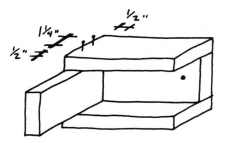

☐ Turn the wall mount over and drive two nails into the other side.

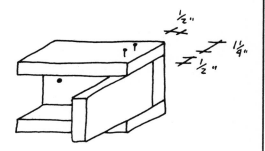

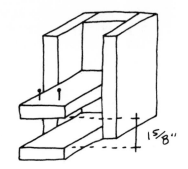

- [ ] Spread a second ¾-inch-wide line of glue inside the wall mount 1⅝ inches above the bottom bar holder. (The 1⅝ inch measurement for this piece may vary according to the actual dimension of your 1 x 2. Use the actual width of your 1 x 2 as the size for this measurement.)
- [ ] Slip a prenailed 4-inch-long piece into place as shown.

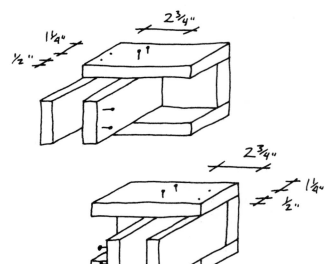

- [ ] Turn the wall mount onto its side and drive two nails through it into the bar holder. Make sure that the distance between the two bar holders is equal to the actual width of your 1 x 2.

68

- [ ] Turn the wall mount over and drive two nails into the other side.

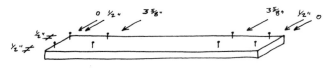

- [ ] Repeat the preceding eight substeps to attach the bar holders to the other wall mount.

Step 5: Attach the towel bar and shelf.

- [ ] Start eight nails into the 18-inch-long 1-x-3-inch piece.

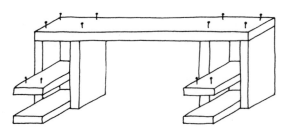

- [ ] Place the two wall mounts on the work surface so that the distance from the outer edge of one to the outer edge of the other is 18 inches.
- [ ] Spread glue on the top edges of both wall mounts.
- [ ] Place the 18-inch-long 1 x 3 on the glued surfaces and nail it into place.

- [ ] Spread glue on the front ¾ inch of the two lower bar holders.

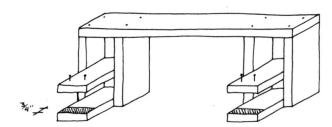

☐ Spread glue on the one ¾-inch edge of the 1-x-2-inch piece as shown.

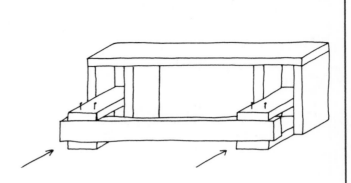

☐ Insert the 1-x-2-inch bar piece between the bar holders and onto the glued surfaces.

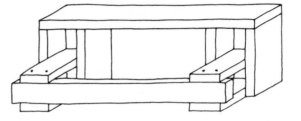

☐ Drive the four nails through the bar holders into the bar piece.

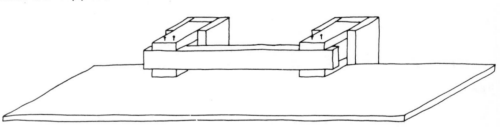

☐ Turn the unit over so that the upper bar supports rest on the edge of the work surface. Drive four nails, two through each bar support, into the bar.

Step 6: **Apply finishing material as desired after the glue has dried. Hang the combination towel bar/shelf on the wall by inserting two screws through the predrilled holes.**

Hanging Instructions

To hang this project on a wood wall, screw flathead wood screws through the "one-by" directly into wood wall. To hang this project on a solid plaster wall, first put plastic or lead plugs, which are available in hardware stores, into the wall and then screw the screws through the "one-by" into the plug. To hang this project on a hollow wall, use molly bolts or toggle bolts (see Glossary).

Design 13:
The Twenty-Four-Inch Towel Bar/Shelf

Materials

Wood	• One 24-inch length of 1-x-2-inch pine
	• One 8-foot length of 1-x-3-inch pine
Nails	• Thirty-six 4-penny finishing nails
Screws	• Two screws for wall attachment
Glue	• Less than one ounce of wood glue
Sandpaper	• One sheet medium-grain sandpaper
	• One sheet fine-grain sandpaper

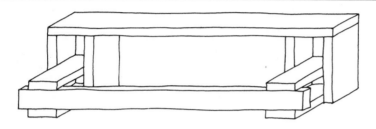

Step 1: Cut wood to size.

☐ One piece of 1-x-2-inch pine 24 inches long.
☐ From the 8-foot length of 1-x-3-inch pine cut one piece 24 inches long, six pieces 6 inches long, and four pieces 4 inches long.

Step 2: Sand wood.

Step 3: Assemble wall mounts.

☐ Start three nails into each of four 6-inch-long pieces.

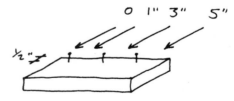

☐ Spread glue along one ¾-inch edge of one of the 6-inch-long pieces that has no nails.

☐ Place one 6-inch-long piece, which has nails started in it, on the glued surface and nail it into position.

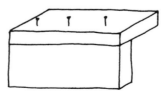

- ☐ Turn the unit over placing the piece just nailed on the work surface. Spread glue on the exposed ¾-inch edge.
- ☐ Place a second prenailed 6-inch-long piece on the glued edge and nail it into position.
- ☐ Drill one hole into the center 6-inch-long piece large enough to accommodate one of the screws you have chosen to fasten the unit to the wall.

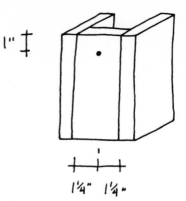

- ☐ Repeat the preceding six substeps to assemble a second wall mount identical to the first.

Step 4: Attach bar holders.

- ☐ Start two nails into two of the four 4-inch-long pieces.

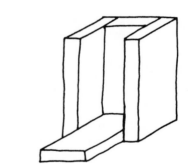

- ☐ Spread glue inside one wall mount at the bottom edge.
- ☐ Slip one of the unnailed 4-inch-long pieces into place as shown.

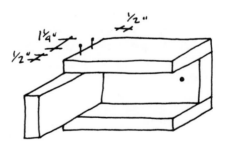

- ☐ Turn the wall mount onto its side and drive two nails through it into the 4-inch-long bar holder.

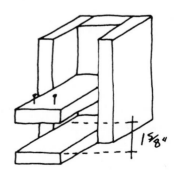

- ☐ Turn the wall mount over and drive two nails into the other side.
- ☐ Spread a second ¾-inch-wide line of glue inside the wall mount 1⅝ inches above the bottom bar holder. (The 1⅝-inch measurement for this piece may vary according to the actual dimension of your 1 x 2. Use the actual width of your 1 x 2 as the size for this measurement.)
- ☐ Slip a 4-inch-long piece, which has nails started in it, into place as shown.

☐ Turn the wall mount onto its side and drive two nails through it into the bar holder. Make sure that the distance between the two bar holders is equal to the actual width of your 1 x 2.

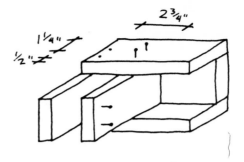

☐ Turn the wall mount over and drive two nails into the other side.

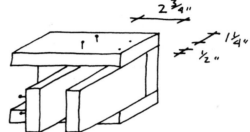

☐ Repeat the preceding eight substeps to attach the bar holders to the other wall mount.

Step 5: Attach the towel bar and shelf.

☐ Start eight nails into the 24-inch-long 1-x-3-inch piece.

☐ Place the two wall mounts on the work surface so that the distance from the outer edge of one to the outer edge of the other is 24 inches.
☐ Spread glue on the top edges of both wall mounts.
☐ Place the 24-inch-long 1 x 3 on the glued surfaces and nail it into place.
☐ Spread glue on the front ¾-inch edge of the two lower bar holders.

☐ Spread glue on one ¾-inch edge of the 1-x-2-inch piece as shown.

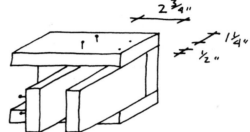

☐ Insert the 1-x-2-inch bar piece between the bar holders and onto the glued surfaces.

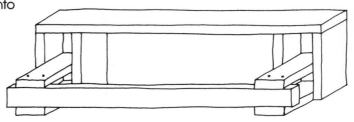

☐ Drive the four nails through the bar holders into the bar piece.

☐ Turn the unit over so that the upper bar supports rest on the edge of the work surface. Drive four nails, two through each bar support, into the bar.

Step 6: Apply finishing material as desired after the glue has dried. Hang the combination towel bar/shelf on the wall by inserting two screws through the predrilled holes.

Hanging Instructions

To hang this project on a wood wall, screw flathead wood screws through the "one-by" directly into wood wall. To hang this project on a solid plaster wall, first put plastic or lead plugs, which are available in hardware stores, into the wall and then screw the screws through the "one-by" into the plug. To hang this project on a hollow wall, use molly bolts or toggle bolts (see Glossary).

Design 14:
The Thirty-Six-Inch Towel Bar/Shelf

Materials

Wood	• One 36-inch length of 1-x-2-inch pine
	• One 8-foot length of 1-x-3-inch pine
Nails	• Thirty-six 4-penny finishing nails
Screws	• Two screws for wall attachment
Glue	• Less than one ounce of wood glue
Sandpaper	• One sheet medium-grain sandpaper
	• One sheet fine-grain sandpaper

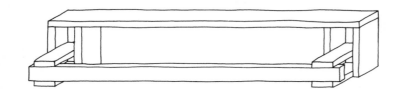

Step 1: Cut wood to size.

☐ One piece of 1-x-2-inch pine 36 inches long.
☐ From the 8-foot length of 1-x-3-inch pine cut one piece 36 inches long, six pieces 6 inches long, and four pieces 4 inches long.

Step 2: Sand wood.

Step 3: Assemble wall mounts.

☐ Start three nails into each of four 6-inch-long pieces.

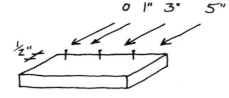

☐ Spread glue along one ¾-inch edge of one of the unnailed 6-inch-long pieces.
☐ Place one 6-inch-long piece, which has nails started in it, on the glued surface and nail it into position.

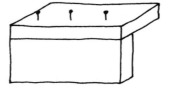

☐ Turn the unit over, placing the piece just nailed on the work surface. Spread glue on the exposed ¾-inch edge.

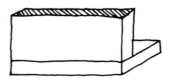

- ☐ Place a second 6-inch-long piece, which has nails started into it, on the glued edge and nail it into position.
- ☐ Drill one hole, large enough to accommodate one of the screws you have chosen to fasten the unit to the wall, into the center 6-inch-long piece.

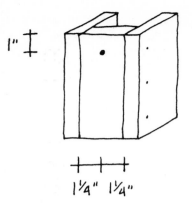

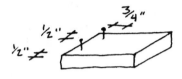

- ☐ Repeat the preceding six substeps to assemble a second wall mount identical to the first.

Step 4: Attach bar holders.

- ☐ Start two nails into two of the four 4-inch-long pieces.

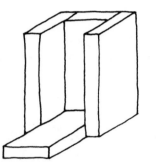

- ☐ Spread glue inside one wall mount at the bottom edge.
- ☐ Slip one of the unnailed 4-inch-long pieces into place as shown.

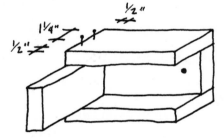

- ☐ Turn the wall mount onto its side and drive two nails through it into the 4-inch-long bar holder.

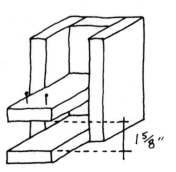

- ☐ Turn the wall mount over and drive two nails into the other side.
- ☐ Spread a second ¾-inch-wide line of glue inside the wall mount 1⅝ inches above the bottom bar holder. (The 1⅝-inch measurement for this piece may vary according to the actual dimension of your 1 x 2. Use the actual width of your 1 x 2 as the size for this measurement.)
- ☐ Slip a prenailed 4-inch-long piece into place as shown.

☐ Turn the wall mount onto its side and drive two nails through it into the bar holder. Make sure that the distance between the two bar holders is equal to the actual width of your 1 x 2.

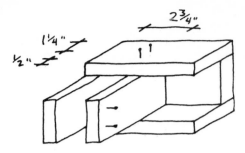

☐ Turn the wall mount over and drive two nails into the other side.

☐ Repeat the preceding eight substeps to attach the bar holders to the other wall mount.

Step 5: Attach the towel bar and shelf.

☐ Start eight nails into the 36-inch-long 1-x-3-inch piece.

☐ Place the two wall mounts on the work surface so that the distance from the outer edge of one to the outer edge of the other is 36 inches.
☐ Spread glue on the top edges of both wall mounts.
☐ Place the 36-inch-long 1 x 3 on the glued surfaces and nail it into place.
☐ Spread glue on the front ¾ inch of the two lower bar holders.
☐ Spread glue on one ¾-inch edge of the 1-x-2-inch piece as shown.

☐ Insert the 1-x-2-inch bar piece between the bar holders and onto the glued surfaces.

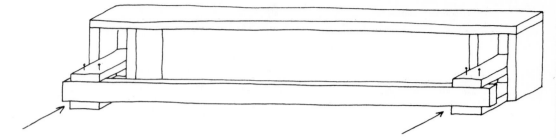

☐ Drive the four nails through the bar holders into the bar piece.

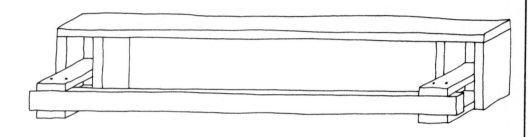

☐ Turn the unit over so that the upper bar supports rest on the edge of the work surface. Drive four nails, two through each bar support, into the bar.

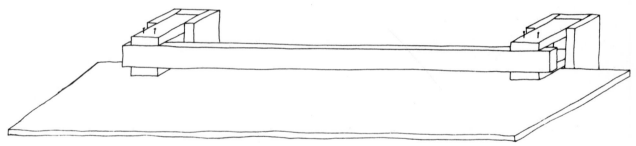

Step 6: Apply finishing material as desired after the glue has dried. Hang the combination towel bar/shelf on the wall by inserting two screws through the predrilled holes.

Hanging Instructions

To hang this project on a wood wall, screw flat-head wood screws through the "one-by" directly into wood wall. To hang this project on a solid plaster wall, first put plastic or lead plugs, which are available in hardware stores, into the wall and then screw the screws through the "one-by" into the plug. To hang this project on a hollow wall, use molly bolts or toggle bolts (see Glossary).

Design 15:
Wall Hooks

Materials

Wood	• One 6-foot length of 1-x-3-inch pine
Nails	• Twenty-eight 4-penny nails
Screws	• Two 2-inch screws (for hanging the hooks)
Glue	• Less than one ounce of wood glue
Sandpaper	• One sheet of medium-grain sandpaper
	• One sheet of fine-grain sandpaper

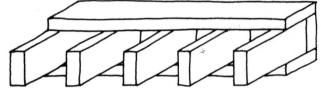

Step 1: Cut wood to size.

☐ From the 6-foot length of 1-x-3-inch pine cut five pieces 4½ inches long and three pieces 15¾ inches long.

Step 2: Sand the wood.

Step 3: Mark lines.

☐ Mark eight lines across each of the three 15¾-inch-long pieces.

Step 4: Start nails.

☐ Start ten nails into each of two of the 15¾-inch-long pieces on the side opposite the lines.

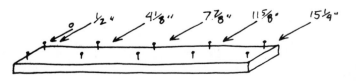

☐ Start four additional nails into each of the same two 15¾-inch-long pieces.

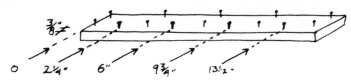

Step 5: Assemble wall hooks.

☐ Spread glue along one ¾-inch-wide edge of the unnailed 15¾-inch-long piece.

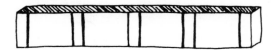

☐ Place one of the other 15¾-inch-long pieces across the glued surface so that the four edge nails are aiming into the lower piece.

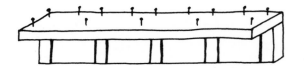

☐ Drive the four edge nails to secure the pieces to one another.

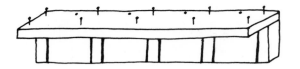

☐ Spread the glue on two edges of one of the 4½-inch-long pieces in the areas shown.

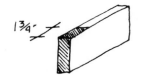

☐ Inside one corner at one end place the glued surfaces against the two 15¾-inch-long pieces that are nailed together.

☐ Drive the two nails to secure the piece in place.

☐ Spread the glue on a second 4½-inch-long piece as above.

1¾"

☐ Place the glued surfaces between the first pair of exposed pencil lines on the 15¾-inch-long pieces and nail the 4½-inch-long piece into position.

☐ One by one, glue and nail the remaining three 4½-inch-long pieces into place. Use the pencil lines as guides for positioning.

☐ Turn the unit over, and spread glue as shown.

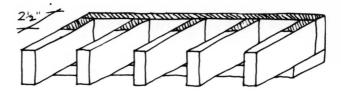

2½"

☐ Place the remaining 15¾-inch-long piece on the glued surface as shown and nail it into place.

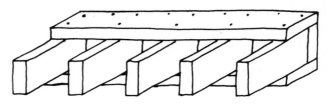

Step 6: Drill holes.

☐ Drill two holes through the back of the wall hooks. The holes should be large enough to accommodate the screws with which you will hang the wall hooks.

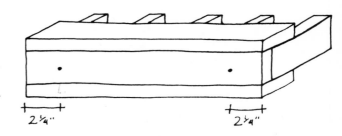

2"

2¼"   2¼"

Step 7: Apply the desired finishing material after allowing the glue to dry thoroughly.

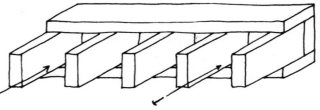

Step 8: Hang the wall hooks.

Hanging Instructions

To hang this project on a wood wall, screw flat-head wood screws through the "one-by" directly into wood wall. To hang this project on a solid plaster wall, first put plastic or lead plugs, which are available in hardware stores, into the wall and then screw the screws through the "one-by" into the plug. To hang this project on a hollow wall, use molly bolts or toggle bolts (see Glossary).

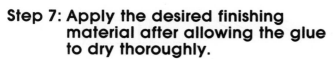

Design 16:
The Letter Holder

Materials

Wood	• One 6-foot length of 1-x-2-inch pine
	• Four 1¼-inch wire brads
Nails	• Twenty-eight 4-penny finishing nails
Glue	• Less than one ounce of wood glue
Sandpaper	• One sheet medium-grain sandpaper
	• One sheet fine-grain sandpaper

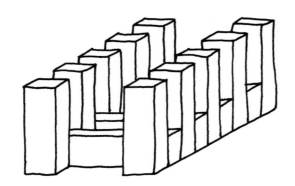

Step 1: Cut wood to size.

☐ Ten pieces, 4½ inches long each
☐ Four pieces, 6¼ inches long each

Step 2: Sand wood.

Step 3: Start nails.

☐ Start four 1¼-inch wire brads into one 6¼-inch-long piece, as shown, two at each end.

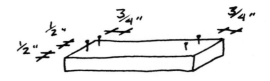

☐ Start four 4-penny nails into the remaining three 6¼-inch-long pieces, as shown, two at each end.

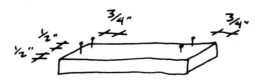

☐ Start two 4-penny nails into eight 4½-inch-long pieces as shown.

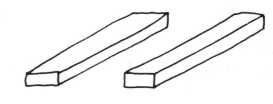

Step 4: Glue and assemble.

☐ Position the two unnailed pieces on the work surface parallel to one another 6¼ inches apart.

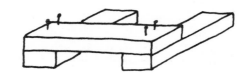

☐ Spread glue on the bottom 1½ inches of both pieces.

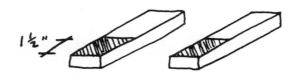

☐ Place the piece with the 1¼-inch wire brads on the glued surfaces and nail it into position. Make sure that the pieces remain at right angles to one another while nailing.

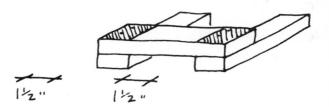

☐ Spread glue on 1½ inches of both ends of the piece that you have just nailed into position.

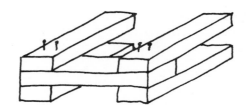

☐ One at a time, place two pieces with two 4-penny nails in each on the glued surfaces and nail them into place. Make sure that they remain at right angles to the piece below while nailing.

☐ Spread glue on the bottom 1½ inches of both pieces that you have just nailed into position.

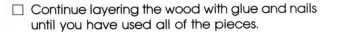
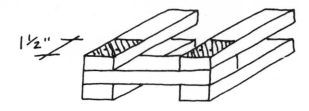

☐ Place one piece with four nails in it across the glued surfaces and nail it into position.

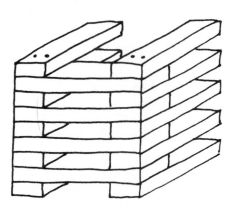

☐ Continue layering the wood with glue and nails until you have used all of the pieces.

Step 5: Apply finishing materials as desired after the glue has dried.

Design 17:

The Wine Rack

Materials

Wood	• Eighteen 6-foot lengths of 1-x-2-inch pine
	• One 10-foot length of 1-x-2-inch pine
Nails	• Four hundred and eighty 1¼-inch wire brads
Glue	• Approximately three ounces of wood glue
Sandpaper	• Two sheets of medium-grain sandpaper
	• Two sheets of fine-grain sandpaper

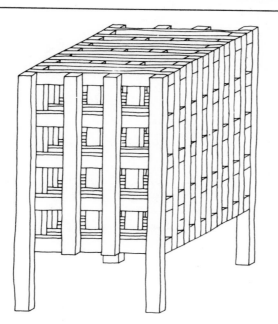

Step 1: Cut wood to size.

☐ From the 10-foot length cut four pieces, each 29 inches long.

☐ From each of eight 6-foot lengths cut three pieces, 22⅛ inches long each.

☐ From each of ten 6-foot lengths cut four pieces, 17 inches long each.

Step 2: Sand wood.

Step 3: Mark lines.

☐ Draw nine pencil lines across two of the four 29-inch-long pieces.

0   1⅝"   5⅛"   6¾"   10¼"   11⅞"   15⅜"   17"   20½"   22⅛"

☐ Draw eight pencil lines across twenty-two of the twenty-four 22⅛-inch-long pieces.

☐ Draw six pencil lines across twenty of the forty 17-inch-long pieces.

Step 4: Start nails.

☐ Start ten nails into the two unmarked 29-inch-long pieces.

☐ Start ten nails into the two unmarked 22⅛-inch-long pieces.

☐ Start ten nails into twenty of the marked 22⅛-inch-long pieces.

☐ Start eight nails into twenty unmarked 17-inch-long pieces.

☐ Start four nails into the twenty marked 17-inch-long pieces.

Step 5: Assemble the wine rack.

☐ Position the two marked 29-inch-long pieces and two marked 22⅛-inch-long pieces (un-nailed) on the work surface parallel to one another, as shown, for the first layer.

☐ Spread glue between the top end of each piece and the first line of pencil marks.

☐ Position one of the 17-inch-long pieces that has eight nails started in it across the glued surfaces for one piece of the second layer.

☐ Nail that 17-inch-long piece into place. While nailing make sure that the pieces remain in place, aligned, and parallel.

☐ Spread glue on the four areas near the other end between the bottom pairs of pencil marks on the outer pieces and the bottom marks and ends of the inner pieces.

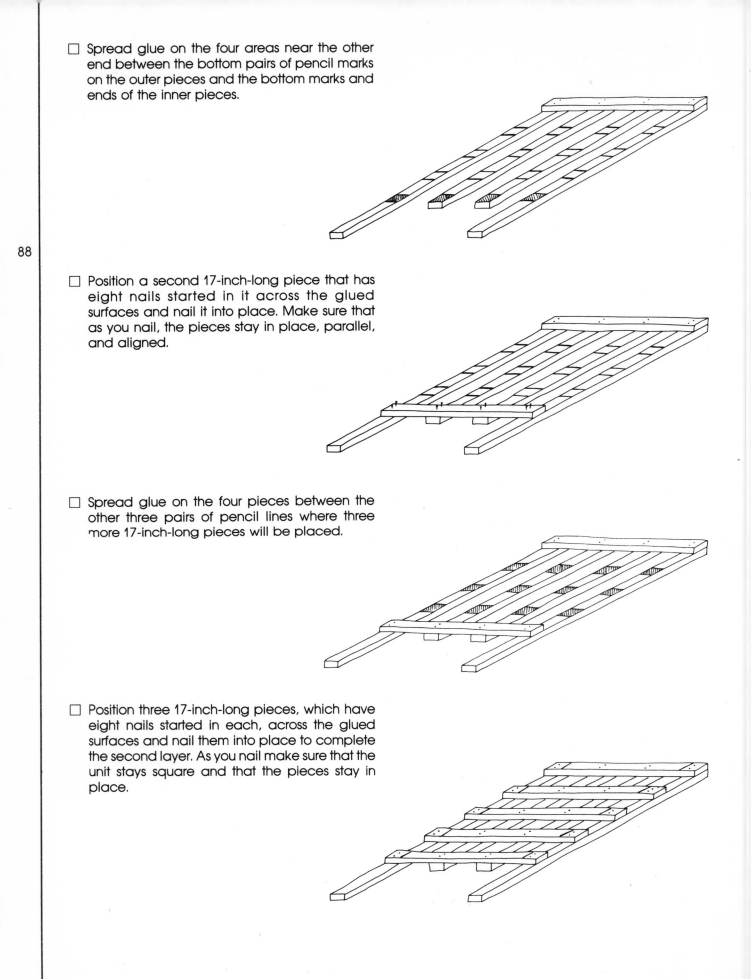

☐ Position a second 17-inch-long piece that has eight nails started in it across the glued surfaces and nail it into place. Make sure that as you nail, the pieces stay in place, parallel, and aligned.

☐ Spread glue on the four pieces between the other three pairs of pencil lines where three more 17-inch-long pieces will be placed.

☐ Position three 17-inch-long pieces, which have eight nails started in each, across the glued surfaces and nail them into place to complete the second layer. As you nail make sure that the unit stays square and that the pieces stay in place.

☐ Spread glue on each end of the five 17-inch-long pieces that you have just nailed into place. The glue covers an area from the end of the piece to 1⅝ inches in from the end.

☐ Place two marked 22⅛-inch-long pieces across the glued surfaces and nail them into place, completing the third layer.

☐ Spread glue in five areas on each of the two 22⅛-inch-long pieces between each end and the innermost pencil marks and between the other three pairs of pencil lines.

☐ Place five 17-inch-long pieces, which have four nails started in each, across the glued surfaces and nail them into place for the fourth layer.

☐ Spread glue in four areas on each of the pieces just nailed in place (at both ends and between the pairs of lines as indicated).

☐ Position four 22⅛-inch-long marked pieces across the glued surfaces and nail them into place for the fifth layer.

☐ Spread glue between the pencil lines and nail five unmarked 17-inch-long pieces into place for the sixth layer.

☐ Spread glue on the five pieces just attached (at both ends, from the end, 1⅝ inches in) and nail two 22⅛-inch-long marked pieces to them for the seventh layer.

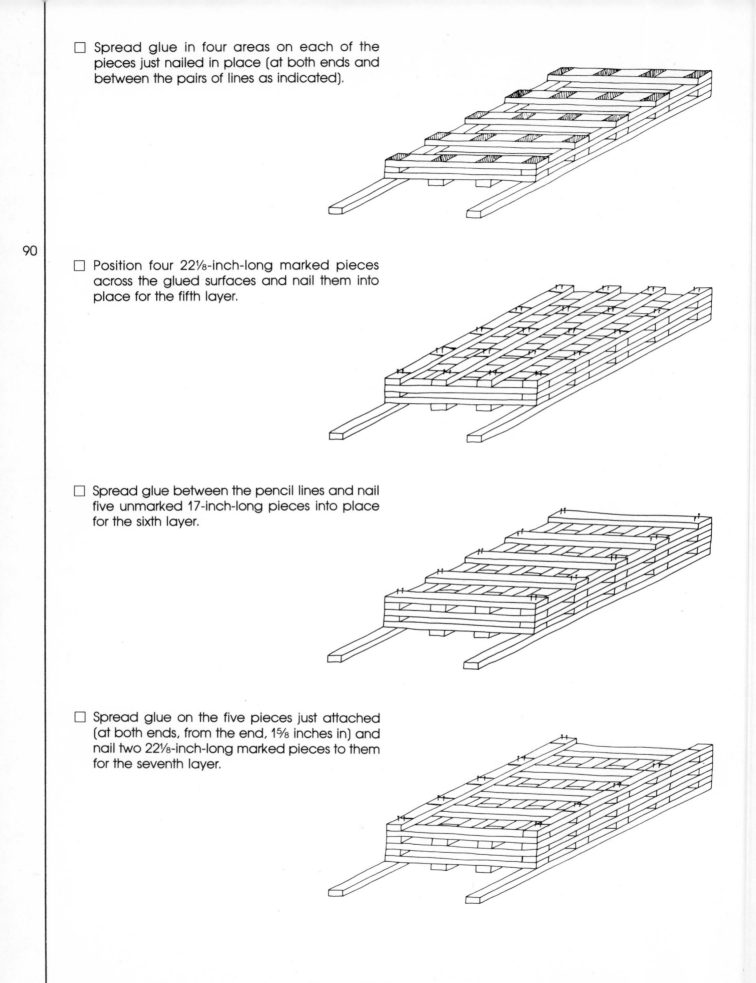

☐ Continue gluing and nailing layers in the following order:

- ☐ eighth layer—five 17-inch-long pieces with four started nails in each.
- ☐ ninth layer—four 22⅛-inch-long marked pieces.
- ☐ tenth layer—five 17-inch-long unmarked pieces.
- ☐ eleventh layer—two 22⅛-inch-long marked pieces.
- ☐ twelfth layer—five 17-inch-long marked pieces.
- ☐ thirteenth layer—four 22⅛-inch-long marked pieces.
- ☐ fourteenth layer—five 17-inch-long unmarked pieces.
- ☐ fifteenth layer—two 22⅛-inch-long marked pieces.
- ☐ sixteenth layer—five 17-inch-long marked pieces

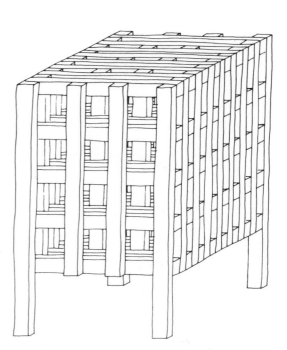

☐ Finish assembly using the four remaining unmarked pieces: two 22⅛-inch-long pieces and two 29-inch-long pieces. In order to make sure that the wine rack will sit flat, position the 29-inch-long pieces and use a hammer to lightly tap them into place. Do not drive the nails completely. If the rack sits flat when you stand it up, finish driving the nails. If it doesn't sit flat, remove the 29-inch-long pieces one at a time. While the unit is standing, reposition them until the four 29-inch-long pieces rest squarely on the flat surface. Then drive the nails.

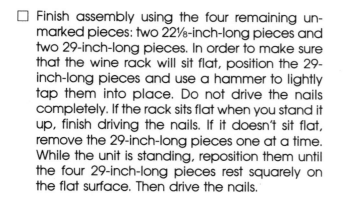

Step 6: Allow the glue to dry thoroughly, at least twelve hours.

Step 7: Apply finishing material as desired.

Design 18:
The Coat Stand

Materials

Wood	• Fourteen 6-foot lengths of 1-x-2-inch pine
	• Four 10-foot lengths of 1-x-2-inch pine
Nails	• Two hundred and forty 1¼-inch wire brads
Glue	• Approximately three ounces of wood glue
Sandpaper	• Two sheets of medium-grain sandpaper
	• Two sheets of fine-grain sandpaper

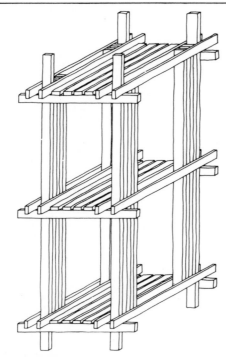

Step 1: Cut the wood to size.

☐ From each of four 6-foot lengths cut one piece 71 inches long.

☐ From each of six 6-foot lengths cut three pieces, each 22½ inches long.

☐ From each of three 6-foot lengths cut four pieces, each 16½ inches long.

☐ From one 6-foot length cut three pieces, each 16½ inches long.

☐ From each of four 10-foot lengths cut two pieces, each 59 inches long.

Step 2: Sand the wood.

Step 3: Assemble the side units.

☐ With a pencil lightly mark twelve lines across six of the 22½-inch-long pieces.

☐ Start twelve nails into each of the same six 22½-inch-long pieces on the side opposite the pencil lines.

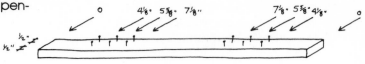

☐ Mark six lines across both ¾-inch edges of the two 71-inch-long pieces.

☐ Position the two 71-inch-long pieces and four 59-inch-long pieces on the work surface parallel to one another as shown.

☐ Spread glue between the bottom pairs of pencil lines on the two 71-inch-long pieces and in an area from the bottom end to 1⅝ inches from the bottom end on the four 59-inch-long pieces.

☐ Place one prenailed 22½-inch-long piece across the glued surfaces and nail it into position. Use the lines on the underside of the 22½-inch-long pieces for exact placement. As you nail make sure that the pieces stay square, parallel, and aligned.

☐ Spread glue between the top pairs of pencil lines on both 71-inch-long pieces and in an area from the top end to 1⅝ inches from the end on the four 59-inch-long pieces.

☐ Place a second prenailed 22½-inch-long piece across the glued surfaces and nail it into position. Use the lines on the underside of the 22½-inch-long piece as guides for placement. As you nail make sure that the pieces stay square and parallel.

☐ Spread glue between the center pair of pencil lines on the two 71-inch-long pieces and in areas covering 1⅝ inches on the four 59-inch-long pieces between the outer areas of glue.

☐ Place a third 22½-inch-long piece across the glued surfaces using the lines on the underside as guides. Nail it into position.

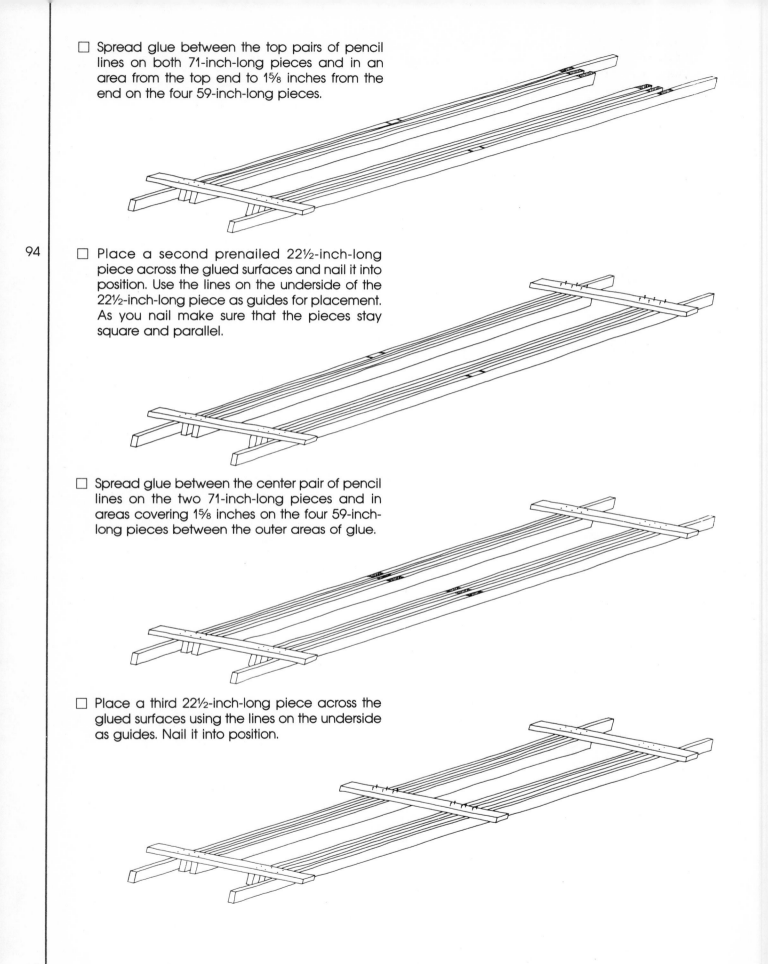

☐ Turn the unit over and repeat the preceding six substeps to attach three more 22½-inch-long pieces to the other side of it as indicated by the pencil lines on the 71-inch- and 22½-inch-long pieces.

☐ Repeat all of Step 3 to build a second side unit identical to the first.

Step 4: Connect the two side units.

☐ Mark four lines across six of the 22½-inch-long pieces.

☐ Start six nails into each of the six 22½-inch-long pieces on the side opposite the pencil marks.

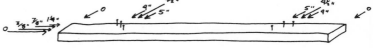

☐ Spread glue in two areas on one of the 22½-inch-long pieces in areas defined by the pencil marks.

☐ Place the two side units on the work surface parallel to one another so that the distance from the outer edge of the 71-inch-long pieces of one unit to the outer edge of the 71-inch-long pieces of the other unit is 15 inches. (Unless the 22½-inch-long pieces of the side unit are perfectly aligned, the side units will not stand on edge by themselves. In order to simplify the logistics of assembly, you should have someone hold the units up until they are nailed together.

☐ Place the glued surfaces of the 22½-inch-long piece across the side units—using the lines that outline the glued areas as guides for placement—just beneath and touching the bottom sets of 22½-inch-long pieces of the side units. Nail the piece into position.

☐ Spread glue on a second 22½-inch-long piece as above.

☐ Place the glued surface of the 22½-inch-long piece across the side units just below and touching the top sets of 22½-inch-long pieces on the side units and nail it into position.

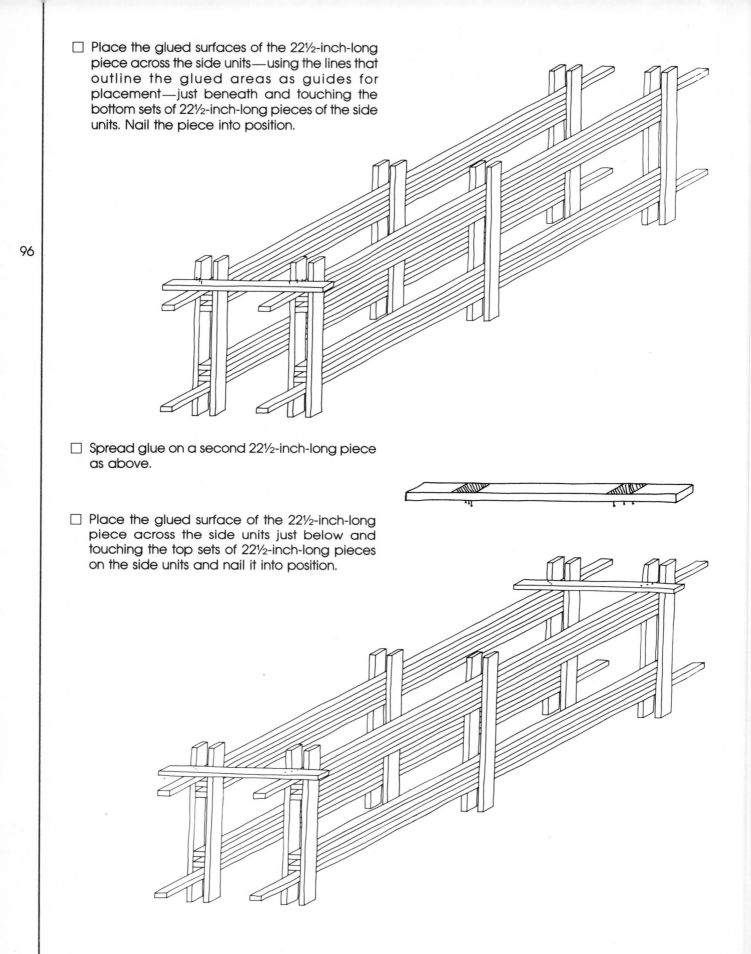

□ Glue and nail a third 22½-inch-long piece across the side units just beneath and touching the middle set of 22½-inch-long pieces of the side units.

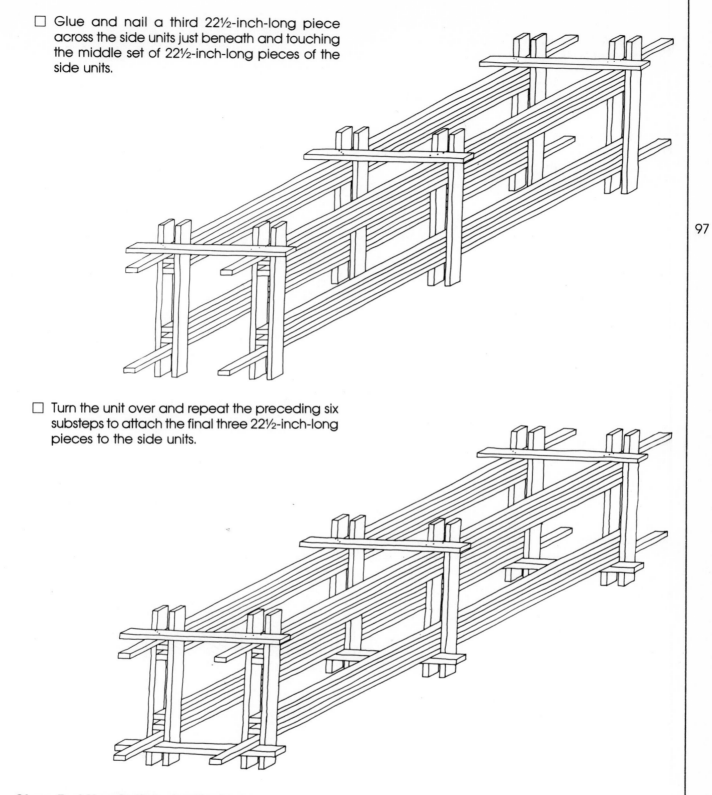

□ Turn the unit over and repeat the preceding six substeps to attach the final three 22½-inch-long pieces to the side units.

Step 5: Attach the shelf pieces.

□ Start four nails into each of the fifteen 16½-inch-long pieces.

☐ Spread glue on one of the 16½-inch-long pieces at the two ends on the side opposite the started nails.

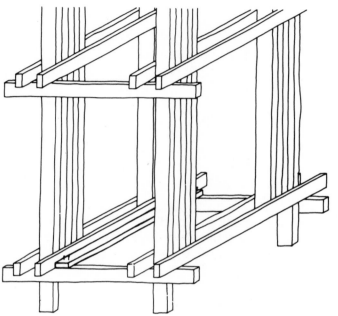

☐ Place the glued edges of the 16½-inch-long pieces across the lower 22½-inch-long pieces that were attached in Step 4. Nail the piece into position so that one of its edges touches one of the 22½-inch-long pieces of the side unit.

☐ Spread glue on a second 16½-inch-long piece as before and nail it across the lower 22½-inch-long pieces so that one edge touches the 22½-inch-long piece of the outer side unit.

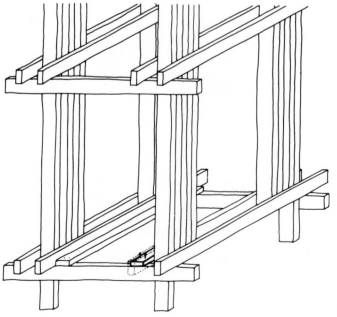

☐ One by one, glue and nail three more 16½-inch-long pieces between the first two with spaces of approximately ½ inch between each.

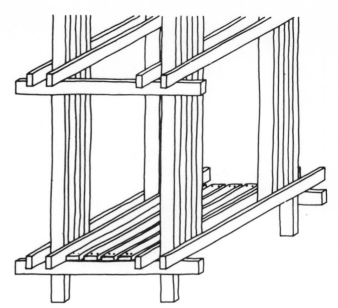

☐ To create a top and a middle shelf, repeat the preceding four substeps twice to glue and nail the remaining ten 16½-inch-long pieces into place.

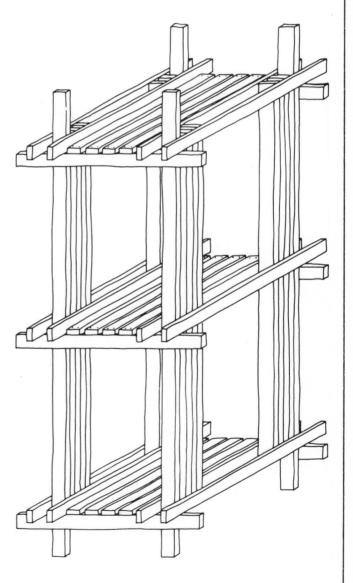

Step 6: Allow the glue to dry thoroughly, for at least 12 hours.

Step 7: Apply desired finishing material.

ACCESSORIES

Design 19:
The Dressing Screen

Materials (for 3 panels)

Wood	• Eleven 8-foot lengths of 1-x-4-inch pine
	• Three 10-foot lengths of 1-x-2-inch pine
Nails	• Forty-two 1¼-inch wire brads
Glue	• Wood glue (approximately three ounces)
Hardware	• Six screw eyes and six screw hooks
Sandpaper	• One sheet medium-grain sandpaper.
	• One sheet fine-grain sandpaper.

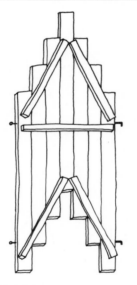

Step 1: Cut wood to size.

☐ From the 1-x-4-inch length cut 21 pieces, 46 inches long.

☐ From the three 10-foot lengths of 1-x-2-inch pine cut 15 pieces, 23¼ inches long.

Step 2: Sand wood.

Step 3: Assemble panels.

☐ Position seven 46-inch-long pieces on the work surface as shown.

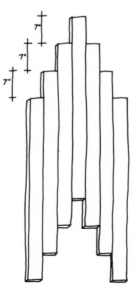

☐ Place five 23¼-inch-long pieces across the 46-inch-long pieces.

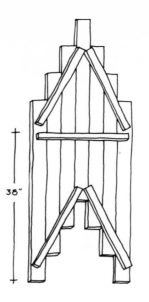

☐ Using a pencil, outline the 23¼-inch-long pieces on the 46-inch-long pieces.

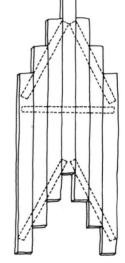

☐ Mark the positioning of nails on the 23¼-inch-long pieces. Two nails will go into each 23¼-inch-long piece where it crosses a 46-inch-long piece.

☐ Remove the 23¼-inch-long pieces from the 46-inch-long pieces and start 1¼-inch wire brads as marked.

☐ Spread glue on the 46-inch-long pieces as marked.

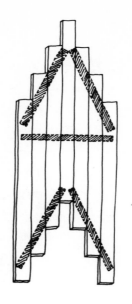

☐ One by one, reposition the five 23¼-inch-long pieces on the glued surfaces and nail them into place.

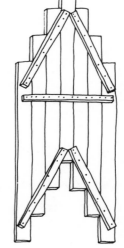

☐ Repeat to assemble two more panels. (Each additional panel requires three and one-half lengths of 8-foot-long 1-x-4-inch pine and one 10-foot length of 1-x-2-inch pine.)

38″   38½″

7″   7½″

Step 4: Attach hardware.

☐ Screw two screw eyes and two L-hooks into each panel.

Design 20:
The Plant Box

Materials

Wood • Five 6-foot lengths of 1-x-2-inch pine
Nails • Eighty-eight 1¼-inch wire brads
Glue • Approximately two ounces of wood glue
Sandpaper • One sheet of medium-grain sandpaper
• One sheet of fine-grain sandpaper

Step 1: Cut wood to size.

☐ From each of four 6-foot lengths cut five pieces, two 12⅞ inches long and three 14¼ inches long.

☐ From one 6-foot length cut four 14¼-inch-long pieces.

Step 2: Sand the wood.

Step 3: Assemble the base.

☐ Mark ten lines across one ¾-inch edge of two of the 12⅞-inch-long pieces.

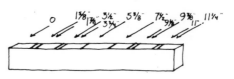

☐ Mark four lines across one side of six of the 14¼-inch-long pieces.

☐ Start four nails into each of the six marked 14¼-inch-long pieces on the side opposite the lines.

☐ Place the two marked 12⅞-inch-long pieces on the work surface parallel to one another so that the distance from the outer edge of one to the outer edge of the other is 12¾ inches.

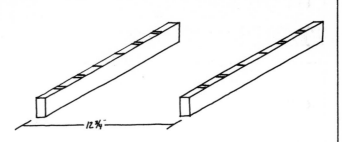

☐ Spread glue on one end of both 12⅞-inch-long pieces from the end to the first pencil line.

☐ Place one of the prenailed 14¼-inch-long pieces across the glued surfaces. Use the lines on the underside of the 14½-inch-long piece as guides for placement and nail the piece to the pieces underneath it. As you work make sure that the pieces stay square, parallel, and aligned.

☐ Spread glue on the other end of both 12⅞-inch-long pieces between the end and the first pencil lines.

☐ Place a second prenailed 14¼-inch-long piece across the glued surfaces and nail it into position. As you nail make sure that the pieces stay square and parallel.

☐ Glue and nail four more prenailed 14¼-inch-long pieces to the 12⅞-inch-long pieces, positioned as indicated by the lines.

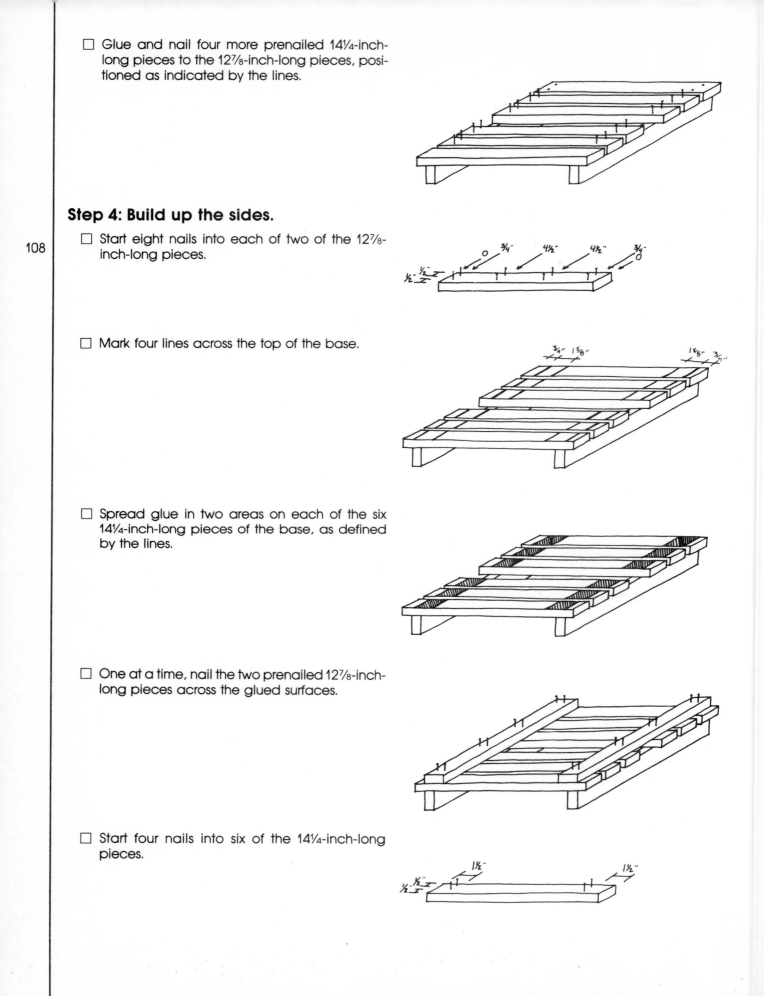

Step 4: Build up the sides.

☐ Start eight nails into each of two of the 12⅞-inch-long pieces.

☐ Mark four lines across the top of the base.

☐ Spread glue in two areas on each of the six 14¼-inch-long pieces of the base, as defined by the lines.

☐ One at a time, nail the two prenailed 12⅞-inch-long pieces across the glued surfaces.

☐ Start four nails into six of the 14¼-inch-long pieces.

☐ Start four nails into four of the 12⅞-inch-long pieces.

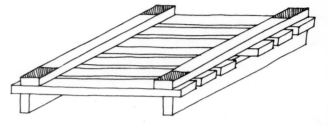

☐ Spread glue at both ends of both 12⅞-inch-long pieces nailed to the top of the base. The glue area extends from the end in 1⅝ inches.

☐ One at a time, nail two 14¼-inch-long pre-nailed pieces across the glued surfaces.

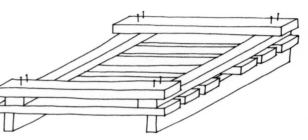

☐ Spread glue on both ends of both 14¼-inch-long pieces that were just nailed in place. The glue area extends from ¾ inch in from the end to 2⅜ inches from the end.

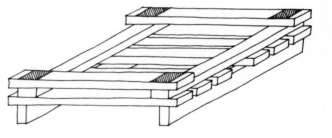

☐ One at a time, nail two prenailed 12⅞-inch-long pieces across the glued surfaces. The edges of the 12⅞-inch-long pieces are ¾ inch in from the ends of the 14¼-inch-long pieces.

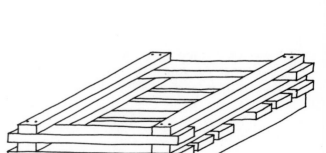

☐ Continue layering the pieces with glue and prenailed pieces in the following order until you have used up all the prenailed pieces: (1) two 14¼-inch-long pieces, (2) two 12⅞-inch-long pieces, (3) two 14¼-inch-long pieces.

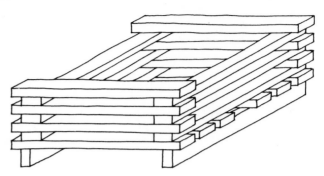

Step 5: Assemble the handle.

☐ Start four nails, two at each end, into two of the 14¼-inch-long pieces.

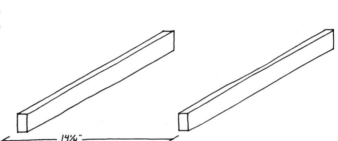

☐ Place two unnailed 14¼-inch-long pieces on the work surface parallel to one another. The distance from the outer edge of one to the outer edge of the other should be 14¼ inches.

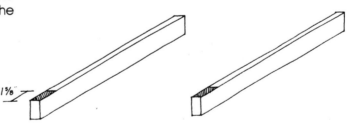

☐ Spread glue on one area on each of the pieces from one end to 1⅝ inches in from the end.

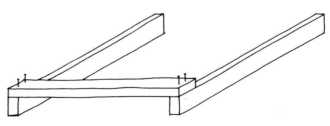

☐ Place one of the prenailed 14¼-inch-long pieces across the glued surfaces and nail it into place. As you nail make sure that the pieces stay square, parallel, and aligned.

☐ Turn the unit over and glue and nail the second prenailed 14¼-inch-long piece to the other side.

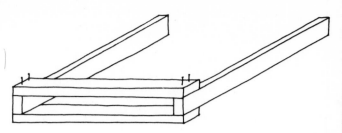

Step 6: Attach the handle.

☐ Rest the basket on its side as shown and mark two lines across the outside of the bottom 12⅞-inch-long pieces.

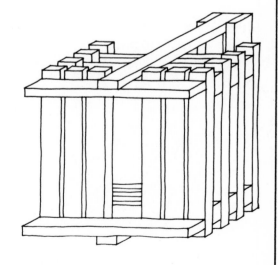

☐ Spread glue on both 12⅞-inch-long pieces between the lines.

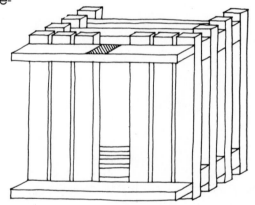

☐ Slide the handle into position.

☐ Drive four nails through the handle into the base.

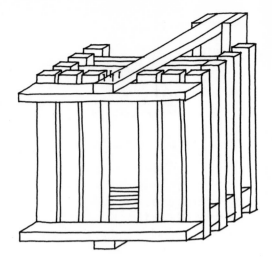

☐ Turn the unit over and drive four nails through the other side of the handle into the base.

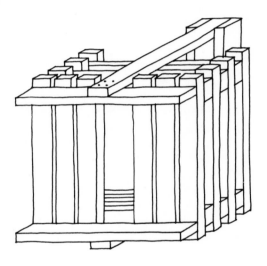

Step 7: Allow the glue to dry thoroughly, for at least twelve hours.

Step 8: Apply the finishing material of your choice.

Glossary

Actual Dimension—The true size of wood as sold by lumberyards. Wood is ordered by length, thickness, and width. When ordering wood you might, for example, need 8 feet of 1 x 4. The piece of wood that you receive should be 8 feet long; however, it will be ¾ inch thick and 3½ inches wide. For a complete listing of actual dimensions for various wood sizes, refer to the Carpentry Guide.

Backsaw—A small handsaw with a reinforced back edge that keeps the blade rigid. The teeth of this saw are finer than on a normal crosscut saw, allowing it to cut exceedingly smoothly. It is excellent for use with a miter box.

Carpenter's Glue—Adhesive that is specially formulated for woodworking. Most white glues, such as Elmer's or Sobo, will do a perfectly adequate job for the projects in this book. However, I generally use "Elmer's Professional Carpenter's Wood Glue," which is available in most hardware stores and lumberyards.

Carpenter's Level—An instrument, generally made of wood or aluminum, which contains liquid-filled, slightly curved vials. The liquid-filled vials contain an air bubble, which, when centered between two lines on the vial, indicate absolute flatness or verticality. Most "combination squares" have built-in carpenter's levels.

Carriage Bolt—A screw-type fastener that is used in conjunction with a nut. The head of the bolt is round and convex. Beneath the head is a shoulder that keeps the bolt from turning after it has been tightened.

Caster—A wheel, or a set of wheels, that attaches to the bottom of a piece of furniture to permit it to roll.

Clear Pine—Wood from a pine tree that is free of virtually any knots or blemishes. Clear wood generally comes from the section of the tree just inside the bark.

Combination Square—An adjustable tool for marking right-angle cuts and testing adjoining members for squareness. The combination square consists of a metal ruler and a metal right-angle clamp that can slide up and down on the ruler. The right-angle clamp usually contains a level.

Crosscut Saw—A handsaw for cutting across the grain of a piece of wood.

Dowel—A round wooden pin that fits into holes in adjoining pieces to keep them from slipping.

"Dressed Four Sides"—Lumber that has had its four large surfaces planed smooth.

Finishing Nail—A nail with a very small head that is intended for use on furniture, cabinet work, and moldings.

Hand Drill—A manually operated tool for making small round holes.

Handsaw—A manually operated tool that has a blade with sharp teeth for cutting.

L-Bent Screw Hook—A single rod of metal in which one end is a screw and the other end is bent to form a 90-degree angle to the screw end.

Miter Box (also, Mitre Box)—A three-sided wood or metal device used to hold a piece of wood and guide a saw while cutting. The miter box is used for straight (90-degree) cuts and 45-degree angle cuts.

Molly Bolt—A device used to fasten into a hollow wall. The molly bolt is pushed through a predrilled hole in the wall; as it is tightened with a screwdriver, its legs spread to grasp the inside of the wall.

Nail Set—A metal tool used to drive the head of a finishing nail below the surface of the wood.

Nominal Dimension—The size of wood as it is commonly referred to and as it comes from the lumber mill's saw. When wood reaches the consumer, it is somewhat smaller than its nominal dimension due to shrinkage in drying and planing in smoothing operations. For example, a piece of wood with a nominal dimension of 1 x 4 has an actual dimension of ¾ x 3½".

Number Two Pine—Wood from a pine tree that has some knots but should still be structurally sound.

Opacity—The degree to which you can see through a material. If you paint a piece of very grainy or marked-up wood with a paint color that has low opacity, you will be able to see the grain or marks through the paint. If you paint with a color or type of paint with higher opacity, that paint will hide what is beneath it.

Penny—A designation of nail size. Derived originally from the price of nails per hundred, the term now signifies only length. Nails are generally available in sizes from 2-penny (abbreviated 2d), which is one inch long, to 60-penny, which is six inches long.

Perfect Glue Joint—A connection of two pieces of wood in which the area of the point of meeting is entirely covered with glue.

Piano Hinge (also, Continuous Hinge)—A long, narrow hinge used when full support of a door or lid is required. Most commonly used for piano lids, the piano hinge is also used for cabinet doors, chests, and small storage boxes. It can be made of steel, aluminum, brass, or nickel and comes in easy-to-cut lengths up to seven feet.

Plastic Wood (trade name)—A claylike substance used to fill wood in order to conceal countersunk nail heads, cracks, or seams in wood. Plastic Wood is applied and smoothed with a putty knife. Once it dries and hardens after application, it can be sanded and accepts finishing material much as wood does. It is available in several wood colors for use under clear finishes.

Polyurethane Varnish—A clear, durable, easy-to-apply, plastic-base finishing material.

Power Drill—A motorized tool for making small round holes.

Power Saw—A motorized tool that has a blade with sharp teeth for cutting. Power saws are made in a hand-held model, known as a "circular power saw," and a table-mounted model, known as a "bench saw" or a "table saw."

Primer—The first coat (or undercoat) of finishing material that is put directly onto the surface being finished. When painting wood, the primer will fill small cracks and begin to cover marks and grain lines before you apply more expensive paint. A primer is especially useful under paint that has low opacity.

Rip Saw—A hand or power saw designed to cut parallel to the grain of wood.

Sandpaper—Paper or cloth that is coated with abrasive material used for removing splinters, marks, roughness, ridges, or sharp corners from wood and other materials. It ranges in grade from very coarse to very fine. Coarse is used to smooth deep scratches and other imperfections. Medium is used for removing surface marks, small scratches, and small ridges. Fine sandpaper is used for final sanding before application of primer or sealer. Very fine sandpaper is used for sanding between coasts of lacquer, varnish, or paint.

Screw Eye—A single rod of metal in which one end is a screw and the other end is bent to form a ring.

Shellac—A wood sealer that is applied under final finish coats to prevent stains on the wood from seeping through the finish coat. Shellac can spoil in its can after only a few months and also, once applied, can develop cracks if used in a moist area. Wherever possible, it might be better to use any one of a number of more up-to-date sealers that are now on the market.

Steel Tape Rule—A long, flexible metal ruler that rolls into a small case.

Table Saw—A power saw in which the round blade protrudes through a slot in the top of a metal table. Wood is passed over the blade for cutting rather than the saw passing over the wood, as with a "circular power saw."

Toggle Bolt—A device used to fasten objects to a hollow wall. The toggle bolt is pushed through a pre-drilled hole in the wall; once it is through the hole, its spring-loaded wings spread. As it is tightened with a screwdriver, the wings clamp against the inside of the wall.

Washer—A flat ring placed between a screw head and the material into which it is attached.

Wing Nut—A metal block with two flat, widely projecting pieces and a threaded hole in the center for screwing it onto a bolt in order to hold things together. The two flat pieces enable the user to tighten it or loosen it by hand, without any other tools.

Wire Brad—A small finishing nail.

Wood Screw—A screw with a sharp pointed tip used to fasten pieces of wood together. A flathead wood screw is for use in a countersunk hole, and its top is flush with the surface of the wood when it is in place. The top of a panhead screw sits on the surface of the wood and looks like a tiny pancake. The top of a roundhead screw sits on the surface of the wood and is dome-shaped.

Peter Stamberg

Peter Stamberg is one of America's leading architectural and furniture designers. Currently Director of Marcatré at Atelier International, he is also known for his designs of residences and commercial spaces. His designs are frequently featured in a wide range of publications, including *The New York Times Magazine, House & Garden, The New York Post,* and *Progressive Architecture.* Mr. Stamberg is the author of *Instant Furniture* and a graduate of Columbia University, the Rhode Island School of Design and The Architectural Association of London. He resides in New York City.